MARKETING
THE
REVOLUTION

CW01067107

MARKETING
THE
REVOLUTION

THE NEW ANTI-CAPITALISM AND
THE ATTACK UPON CORPORATE BRANDS

MICHAEL MOSBACHER

Published by The Social Affairs Unit

British Library Cataloguing in Publication Data
A catalogue record of this book is available from
the British Library

ISBN 0 907631 95 9

Book production and typesetting by Crowley Esmonde Ltd
Printed and bound in Great Britain by Woolnough Bookbinding Ltd.

Contents

Preface and Summary 7

1 The Fall and Rise of Anti-Capitalism 11

2 Anti-Branding:
The Medium and The Message 21

3 The Complex Web of Consumers, Owners, and Funders 35

4 Motives Old and New:
Companies as Targets for Protest 47

5 The Fallacies of Anti-Branding 59

6 Brands and The South 71

Biographical Note 77

Notes and references 79

Preface and Summary

After the collapse of the Soviet bloc, capitalism was acknowledged to be the only way of organising a successful economy - at least for a brief time. But by the end of the 1990s, capitalism found itself surrounded by a host of increasingly voluble new critics. At least these critics appear to be doing something new. Many of their campaigns do not, at least initially, attack capitalism as a system or general idea, or offer a thought-out better way of organising the economy. They focus on cases of abuse, cases which result, allegedly, from the actions of particular global corporations: the abuse of the environment, the treatment and low pay of workers in the 'South', child labour, the exploitation of women, the degradation of cultures and the imposition of lifestyles through brands. Particular victims are always more sympathetic than abstract ideas and the new critics' use of them has been very successful.

So, how seriously should these new critics of capitalism be treated? In this study, Michael Mosbacher analyses their contentions in depth and finds that a good number of the new critics are doing little that is new. Even their emphasis on individual alleged abuses is, at least in part, not a new end but a new means to galvanize support for the hatred of capitalism. It's the old hatred with new PR.

Mr Mosbacher is particularly interested in their hostility to and use of brands. The new critics make the following contentions:

> They claim to dislike the way brands work but it is brands that have given their own campaigns a new lease of life. In order to attack brands, the critics piggy-back their own anti-capitalist message on to the brands' renown and gain a fresh audience for their views.
>
> They do this while claiming that they, the opponents of the corporations, are denied access to the mainstream media and are made voiceless. This is palpably false. Anti-corporate tracts - such as Naomi Klein's *No Logo*, George Monbiot's *The Captive State*, and the works of Noam Chomsky - have become

bestsellers for mainstream publishers. Hollywood films parrot the anti-corporate message. Anti-branding has entered mass public consciousness in record time. Anti-corporate campaigns even receive funding from media moguls such as Ted Turner.

They claim the corporations allegedly taking over the world are constantly becoming larger. In fact the largest 500 corporations' share of US assets fell by 20 per cent, and their share of all those employed by nearly one third in just over ten years.

They present the world as divided into two opposed, permanently hostile and exclusive parts: consumer-worker victims and their valiant campaigners; and large employer-producer exploiters and their apologists. Yet these corporations have only become what they are today due to the enthusiastic custom of millions of individual consumers. The ownership of these corporations, far from becoming ever more concentrated, has in fact become extremely broad. At the end of 2000, nearly 18 per cent of all UK shares were owned by pension funds and insurance companies owned 21 per cent. This represents the collective savings of millions of ordinary people. Ever more people benefit from the profits of large companies.

Furthermore many of the most vehement anti-corporate campaigners rely on financial support from the corporate and corporate-created wealth they despise, from the likes of Doug Tompkins, the founder of Esprit and The North Face clothing brands, with his Foundation for Deep Ecology, to The Body Shop Foundation, and The Ben & Jerry Foundation.

They argue that globalisation is making the lot of the poor in the South worse. Yet, in general the position of the poor is improving in those countries that are becoming more integrated into the global economy, such as Vietnam and China. Whereas in those countries not becoming more integrated into the world economy, those that are not globalising, such as Zimbabwe and much of the rest of Africa, the position of the poor is static, or worsening.

They imply, by their recitation of particular abuses and attacks upon particular brands that they are concerned with the specific abuses. Yet they often target corporations which are among the most 'ethical' in their policies especially if they have high brand recognition which might give their own anti-capitalism that brand's audience. The leading advocate and chronicler of anti-branding, Naomi Klein, puts it thus: 'For years, we in the movement have fed off our opponents' symbols - their brands, their office towers, their photo-opportunity summits. We have used them as rallying cries, as focal points, as popular education tools. But these symbols were never the real target: they were the levers, the handles.'

What is new about the new critics are their tactics, their use of individual cases and of the media. And even these like so many of their resources are not that original; they came from the working of modern corporate PR. Take away the heartstring 'abuse' cases and the second-hand PR and what is left is little more than a crude and entirely negative hatred of capitalism.

There is no thoughtful analysis of the system they so loathe, no awareness of how they themselves are part of it, no carefully considered alternative for the betterment of the world. Corporations obviously have to take the new critics seriously insofar as their own public relations are concerned, but Mr Mosbacher finds no reason why they or anyone else should take the new critics intellectually seriously.

Social Affairs Unit publications express the views of their authors not those of the Social Affairs Unit, its Trustees, Advisers or officers. However, I can commend this study as a thoughtful contribution to an important public debate.

Digby Anderson, London, 2002

1

The Fall and Rise of Anti-Capitalism

The collapse of the old anti-capitalism

The democratic revolutions in Eastern Europe in 1989 and the collapse of the Soviet Union in 1991 were heralded as marking the unambiguous triumph of both the capitalist system and bourgeois liberal democracy. 'Real existing socialism' had been both practically and morally discredited. Even someone sympathetic to aspects of socialism such as the director of Russian Studies at Princeton, Stephen Kotkin, points out that the planned economy just could not deliver the goods. Rectification was impossible. The Soviet system had 'no mechanisms for self-correction'.[1] Although it was once *de rigueur* for fashionable intellectuals to eulogise and extol the virtues of the Soviet system, as Paul Hollander recounts in *Political Pilgrims: Travels of Western Intellectuals in Search of the Good Society*,[2] 'real existing socialism' as was has few defenders today. The only people to stand up for it now in the West are small groups of ageing men who stick together in Stalinist sects and remember their struggles of yesteryear and their fraternal visits from East European comrades.[3]

It was argued, most famously by Francis Fukuyama in his over-cited *The End of History and the Last Man*,[4] that, with the manifest failure of the socialist experiment, the clash of ideologies was at an end. The broad consensus became that market-based economies had been shown to be the only ones able to deliver their people a better standard of living and bourgeois liberal democracies the only form of government compatible with human decency. The only debates that remained, or so the argument went, were to what extent capitalism ought to be regulated and how those who were unable to provide for themselves ought to be provided for.

To a significant extent this new consensus has survived the last ten years. To generalise, mainstream politics in the West is today, by and large, a discussion of how capitalism ought to be managed and how welfare ought to be provided. Major political parties are not advocating mass nationalisation. Even protest movements now talk the language of capitalism. Instead of proselytising against the evils of capitalism, the established campaigning organisations are more likely to be found holding seminars for the business community extolling the virtues of corporate social responsibility, or arguing that this or that aspect of the global economy ought to be 'reformed' in order to soften its harsher edges. Organisations such as Greenpeace International, while still being highly confrontational towards specific companies when they believe it to be appropriate, also spend much time telling companies that they should embrace environmentally friendly practices, or invest in renewable energy sources or some other 'green' technology, because it is in the companies' own economic interest to do so. Such organisations may not like capitalism, but they see it as 'the only game in town', and thus they can only hope to achieve anything by working within its framework.

The rise of the 'new' anti-capitalism

Over the past five years, however, the Western world has seen the rise of new protest movements that are challenging the ideological settlement that seemed to have emerged by the early 1990s. There have been large, often violent, anti-capitalist demonstrations and street events in most major Western cities. These demonstrations have usually been organised to counter some international financial summit or around some symbolically important day such as the first of May. These new protesters see as their targets what they perceive as the evils of globalisation, the supposed ever-growing reach of corporate power, and the insidious influence of corporate brands. At most, tens of thousands take part in each of these demonstrations. The underlying appeal of their message, however, goes much further than this. The violence of some of the demonstrators may be seen as somewhat extreme, but the fears that animate the demonstrators resonate with many.

The rise of this new protest movement has taken many by surprise. The protesters seem to be articulating a new language of social concern. What is their message? Do they have a new agenda that is radically different from the older anti-capitalist agenda? Or are these new issues simply a repackaging of old arguments? Are they a new marketing device? Today's protesters undoubtedly do not see the former Soviet Union and its satellites as any sort of model. Many do not even reject capitalism in its entirety. That is not the question. What is the question is whether the issues they are campaigning on today, the reasons they hate the market economy as it is currently constituted, are the same ones which animated earlier generations; whether the claims they are making are the ones that experience has shown to be false.

Anti-capitalist protest and the baggage of the past

This is a matter which affects their credibility. But it also affects something else. It is not just a matter of whether the 'new' protest ideology is in fact new but about whether it is based on new cultural impulses. Francois Furet concludes his magisterial study of the attractiveness of Communism by saying that 'the Communist idea will not rise again in the form in which it died . . . [it] has undoubtedly come to an end along with the Soviet Union'.[5] But those words suggest it might return under another guise. And Furet argues that people will be reluctant to accept that the society we have is the best possible. We are reluctant to accept that we are condemned to live in the world as it is. Democracy creates the need for a world beyond itself, a utopia.

If the new protest movements pull at the same heartstrings as the old, then to understand the protesters, it will be necessary to dust off the old analyses of the attractiveness of socialism, especially to intellectuals, and to re-apply these. Thus, for instance, Paul Hollander analyses the 'estrangement' of radicals from their own country, society and economic system.[6] What is it that makes them not only ungrateful to the hand that has fed them with such historically incomparable largesse but full of hate towards it? He looks at the appeal to intellectuals and armchair warriors of 'force', of making history, of tidying up the world, of imposing theories on realities. He looks at their use of false moral equivalence.

At the end of the day the question of the relationship of today's critics of capitalism to yesterday's must substantially change the debate about the worth of their claims. If they are, in part or in whole, the inheritors of yesterday's protests then they are suddenly faced with baggage to defend. They are no longer free spirits to flit here and there denouncing this abuse of labour in India or of that field of crops in Essex. They are part of an historical movement and they have some very questionable and ugly events and tendencies to account for. This needs to be thought about and argued. It is not enough for them simply to argue that earlier attempts to replace capitalism went wrong, or degenerated, at such and such a point, or that earlier rejections of capitalism were not 'true anti-capitalism'. If any lesson can be drawn from history it is surely that utopian claims do not lead to utopian consequences Who is to say this movement will not degenerate, that this movement is the true face of anti-capitalism? Such easy dismissals of the past failures of anti-capitalism ignore the structural factors within non-market systems that led to these failings.

To think about the claims of the anti-capitalist, anti-corporate movement and their supposed novelty, I have deliberately taken those that look the newest and have proved the most attractive, those about brands. Are the claims being made about brands genuinely new, or are they simply a restatement of old, discredited claims about capitalism? Is anti-branding, in fact, simply a marketing exercise? To answer this one must look at the claims of the anti-branders and what their allegations are.

How anti-capitalists see brands

Brands are ubiquitous. Brands such as Coca-Cola, Levi's and McDonald's have even entered everyday language. Wherever one looks - in the high street, in advertising, within television programmes themselves, in the cinema, even in art galleries and at sporting events - brands and their propaganda confront one. These same brands now make their presence known regardless of where one is. MTV and Nike are to be found in London, New York, Moscow, Beijing, Bangkok, and Johannesburg. And where once brands were only the products they sold, they are now much more than that. Trainers are no longer just trainers, soft drinks are no longer just soft drinks, and coffee is no longer just coffee. For the brands do not simply sell a product, they sell a lifestyle. Drink this drink, wear these trainers, use this perfume, and you too will be sexy, young, athletic and western, you too will be glamorous, you too will have a beautiful partner - in short, you too will be happy. The brands manufacture anxieties to sell their products, they spend vast sums to create fashions and trends, and they make us believe that we are somehow not full persons unless we consume their products. The brands have colonised every facet of our lives.

The culture that the brands have created is a wholly materialist one in which people measure their own worth in the image of the corporation, namely by the colour of their money, not the contents of their character.

And what is worse, the brands often sell this materialism as anti-materialism - nicely wrapped up as a facial scrub at £7.99, a self-assembly bookcase at £79.99. And what are the immense profits of the brands, the engines of their growth, built upon? Exploitation - the exploitation of the poor in poor countries, especially women and children, working in the sweatshops and plantations of the South; the exploitation of the poor in rich countries through the casualisation of labour in the North; the exploitation of consumers everywhere who buy the brands' over-priced products in the elusive hope that these products might somehow bring them fulfilment and happiness; and the exploitation of the environment through the production of unnecessary goods.

This would be bad enough on its own. Even worse the brands portray themselves - with vast multi-million dollar budgets - as being caring, concerned and 'on our side'. They have appropriated a vibrant independent culture of rebellion, and turned it into just another sterile sales pitch. More than this, the brands frequently try to associate themselves with progressive causes - gay rights, the empowerment of women, environmental thinking. The brands are cynically seeking to colonise protest culture. They portray themselves as the solution to the problem that they themselves constitute. Their vast advertising budgets on their own would mean that the media could not afford to criticise the brands and the feel-good world view they propagate. What is worse is that the ownership of capital is becoming more and more concentrated and intertwined. The same companies own the news media and the entertainment industry and make vast synergistic profits from merchandising and the brands they build up. They are hardly going to challenge the branded world view from which they profit. We live in a world of synergistic censorship where the mainstream media will do everything to shore up the economic system from which they profit. The only way of combating these brands and their hegemonic world view is to show up the corporations behind them for the exploiters that they really are. In other words, branding is about building positive images around products; anti-branding is about dismantling these images and replacing them with negative ones.

Why and how anti-capitalists attack brands
The above is a snapshot of how the current crop of anti-corporate activists view brands in general. It is obviously a composite picture, but it does sum up the broad thrust of why activists are targeting brands so assiduously. It is why these activists have made their attacks on brands, alongside their attacks on the myriad

international political and financial summits and conferences which they perceive as the incarnation of a global corporate wealth and power grab, the twin pillars and mainstays of their campaigns. The attack on brands is arguably the more important of these pillars, since it has greater popular appeal and is seen as more mainstream. Brands are more visible than the International Monetary Fund, the World Trade Organization or the World Economic Forum and suchlike; these meetings have only emerged from a relative public obscurity to become occasions for major media coverage as a result of anti-capitalist attacks upon them. Publicity is obviously an inherent and essential requirement for a successful brand. This inherent visibility will make attacks upon brands seem more immediate and relevant, and thus have more popular appeal. The actions against international financial summits have come to be seen as extremist by the public due to the highly photogenic antics of what is admittedly a minority of violent, balaclava-wearing, menacing protesters. Anti-branding does not suffer from this image problem, again reinforcing its popular appeal.

While today's anti-corporate activists have common enemies, they are an extremely heterodox lot. They have divergent ideological bases for their views - some are anarchists; others every conceivable shade of green; a few still would describe themselves as Marxist. Most are best described as simply anti-capitalist or anti-corporate, having no clear end-vision of where they want to be, except away from where we are. They talk vaguely of building a more democratic state and society which is responsive to the 'true desires' of 'ordinary people', whatever and whoever these may be, not to corporate interests. This vagueness has been a cause of criticism of some of today's activists, and indeed of exasperation, for such veteran anti-capitalists as the noted British journalist and would-be revolutionary Paul Foot.[7] But regardless of this, today's anti-capitalists are in agreement as to who the enemy is, if not as to what they want once the enemy is defeated. Type the name of any major brand - from The Gap to Starbucks, Levi's to McDonald's – into an Internet search engine, and sites will come up, as often as not above the brands own official sites, attacking that brand for its alleged abuses. These sites are usually slick and well-produced, and are often parodies of the brand's official sites. The anti-branding sites tend to link up to a whole gamut of other sites attacking other brands. For the activists the attraction of this kind of campaigning is that their message can reach a vast global audience. There is the added pleasure, from the activists' point of view, of knowing that this audience is obtained via the name recognition, achieved and maintained at huge expense, of those they are attacking. Nike, for example, keeps itself in public consciousness via an annual advertising budget of over $150 million.[8] The brands are doing the activists' advertising for them; they are obtaining an audience for the anti-capitalist message. All the anti-capitalists, on the other hand, need to get their message across is a second-hand computer, a website, a few design conscious, IT literate activists, and, most importantly, a high profile brand they can parasitically piggy-back their message upon. It means a virtually no-budget campaign can suddenly have a very significant impact. The current anti-branding movement is very much a product of the Internet culture. Its messages could not have reached the vast audiences they have if it were not for the Internet. The protesters talk of censorship by the mainstream media, but they have found a way of circumventing the mainstream media and still obtaining vast audiences.

Of course the new anti-corporate activism does not stop with the Internet. Billboard advertisements are cleverly altered or defaced. The idea is to change what is being advertised from the brand itself to an attack upon that brand, from a consumer product to an attack upon consumerism. Using the imagery of consumerism in an attempt to question consumerism is, of course, not an entirely new phenomenon; it is the basis for such iconic American pop art as Roy Lichtenstein's overblown pastiches on advertising and cartoon strips and Andy Warhol's representation of Campbell's soup tins, or, in Europe, Italian artist Mimmo Rotella's use of advertising posters in his 'socially critical' collages. The difference, however, between this and the work of today's campaigners is that the campaigners are far more self-consciously political. They are not just playing with popular imagery and seeking to raise a few questions, but have a distinct political message to sell. The campaigners are also adept at staging attention-grabbing spectacles and publicity stunts to promulgate their positions. The anti-branders will seek out whatever vehicles are open to them, from pickets outside shops to turning court actions against them into trials of this or that corporation, in order to damage the reputation of the brands they are attacking.

The popularity of anti-branding: The case of Naomi Klein

This anti-branding message does seem to have popular resonance. This does not mean that the brands themselves are losing out, but anti-branding is itself acquiring a positive public image. For all the protesters' talk of censorship and the need to create alternative, Internet-based channels of communication, the anti-branding message has been very successful in breaking through into the mainstream media. A book which can be seen as both the manifesto and history of the anti-branding movement, *No Logo*[9] was in the UK top ten bestsellers list for many weeks[10], usually somewhere between *Men are from Mars, Women are from Venus* and *Dr Atkins' New Diet Revolution*. *No Logo* has also been a major publishing success in the USA and Canada and a top ten bestseller in France.[11] It can be found piled high in airport bookshops next to John Grisham and Jackie Collins, and has been the number one best selling business book in the UK for many months, elbowing aside the usual diet of chief executives' memoirs and guides for aspiring young executives on how to be effective. *No Logo* has been described as 'a movement bible' by the *New York Times* and as 'capturing the *zeitgeist* of the twenty-first century' by that quintessential twenty-first century brand, Amazon.[12] It has been the subject of the cover, and lead article, in *The Economist*.[13] It has even been positively reviewed by image-conscious men's lifestyle magazine, *GQ*.[14] This is no mean achievement for a radical political tract.

No Logo's author, thirty-something, Canadian Naomi Klein, has become something of a poster girl for anti-branding activists, and has been a favoured guest on radio discussions and news programmes. She has been sought out by the media to comment whenever attacks on corporations and their brands make the news. Major advertising agencies have asked Klein to give presentations to their executives. She, however, has refused these offers, feeling they would undermine her credibility.[15] Klein has also been a star turn at the growing number of international anti-corporate gatherings, such as the World Social Forum held in Porto Alegre,[16] a city in Brazil whose local government is seen as something of a role model by many anti-corporate activists. These gatherings are being organised as the antithesis and supposed antidote to the 'neo-liberalism' of mainstream, establishment international gatherings, such as the favourite target of anti-capitalist protesters, the World Economic Forum, usually held in, and associated with, Davos,

Switzerland. However, in 2002, as an act of solidarity for the September 11th attacks on the World Trade Centre, the World Economic Forum was held in New York, less of a role model for anti-corporate types. The 50,000 people attending the World Social Forum, could hear, along with Klein, assorted other heroes of anti-capitalism: French farmer-activist José Bové; South American leftist, populist politicians; 'intellectuals' associated with the high brow French paper, *Le Monde Diplomatique*, who believe their role is to give anti-globalisation theoretical rigour; and, in 2002 as it is an election year, various French Presidential candidates trying to outdo each other in their anti-Americanism.[17] Klein has perhaps become the leading public voice for the younger generation of Anglo-American anti-corporate activists and their anti-branding message. The cynical might suggest that Klein's anti-branding has become itself a brand, with the help of her UK publishers, Flamingo, a brand of News Corp's (and thus Rupert Murdoch's) HarperCollins. To take this analogy further, as with all successful brands, she has her competitors.

Naomi Klein's competitors - Noreena Hertz and George Monbiot

No Logo is not the only recent English language example of anti-corporate polemic becoming a mainstream publishing success. Other publishers have sought to compete for this market by publishing their own similar, and similarly packaged, mass market tracts. Perhaps the best British examples of this are Heinemann's *The Silent Takeover - Global Capitalism and The Death of Democracy*[18] by Noreena Hertz, and Macmillan's *Captive State - The Corporate Takeover of Britain*[19] by George Monbiot. One thing the anti-corporate movement is clearly not suffering from, whatever they themselves might think, is censorship or exclusion from the mainstream, 'capitalist' media.

The success of these anti-corporate books is symptomatic of the popularity of the ideas that underlie them. John Lloyd, the associate editor of the left-of-centre British news magazine *New Statesman*, describing this movement, says 'Very rapidly - the speed perhaps reflecting the avidity with which the media swallow, chew over and regurgitate anything with the label "new" attached - these themes have become part of the mind-set of the educated, especially the young educated, of most wealthy and middle-income countries.'[20] He argues that far from marginalising the anti-corporate movement, it is to a significant extent the mainstream media's interest in it that has brought the politics of protest into the mainstream of current ideas. Whatever the reason may be, many undoubtedly see anti-branding and the ideas behind it, however erroneously, as new, daring, subversive, edgy. In short they are fashionable and popular. This popularity stretches much further than those who are inclined to go on demonstrations. For those who wish to be perceived as bright free-thinkers, who are willing to challenge the orthodoxy, parroting these types of views is almost *de rigueur*. If they want to be perceived as really on the cutting edge, liberally throwing Noam Chomsky into the conversation seems to do the trick.

When discussing *No Logo* and the branding of anti-branding, the British satirical magazine *Private Eye* suggests, 'with its glamorous author and groovy graphics [it] bears as many signs of the brander's stamp as the average tube of toothpaste.' It is easy to dismiss such comments as crass, glib, even sexist, but they do in fact illustrate the nature and techniques of anti-branding activism extremely well. For what the anti-branding movement does is take on board the culture, ethos, language and techniques of branding, and then use these to attack the brands themselves. The anti-branders believe that the consumer brands have appropriated radical ideas to sell their products, so they will appropriate the methods of branding, and the notion that image is everything, to attack the brands. They will not have the brand's budgets, but they will be able to piggyback on the brands' own renown.

2

Anti-Branding: The Medium and The Message

The anti-branding movement believes branding has blurred the boundaries between radicalism and the status quo

Anti-branding activists maintain that certain brands have appropriated for commercial ends the symbolism, imagery, language and culture of rebellion, even of anti-capitalism. There is something to be said for this argument. Many youth-oriented brands obviously use the imagery and music of youthful rebellion. Some brands have, however, sought to go much further than this by associating themselves with the epochal images of anti-capitalism itself. One need only look at the repeated use of the iconic image of Marxist guerrilla Che Guevara in adverts selling everything from vodka to digital television channels to see it. Che Guevara is dead and, it might be said, his battles long over and not very relevant to the campaigns of today's anti-capitalists. But what if the symbols and icons of today's anti-capitalists are appropriated for advertising? That is exactly what the fashion brand Benetton proposed. Subcommandante Marcos is the leader of Mexico's Zapatista National Liberation Army, a fiercely anti-globalisation, anti-capitalist, anti-rich organisation. Marcos himself is always shown wearing a balaclava, with a pipe in his mouth, and an automatic weapon at his side. Naomi Klein describes him as 'the Che Guevara of his generation'.[21] He is the totemic figure for the current generation of protesters. Apparently Benetton has repeatedly offered Subcommandante Marcos lucrative modelling contracts. He has turned them down.[22] This is no isolated occurrence. Ralph Nader, perhaps the best known opponent of corporate America and Green Party presidential candidate in 1996 and 2000, was offered $25,000 to take part in an ironic advertisement for Nike trainers. He too turned the offer down.[23]

The phenomenon is not exclusive to the most obvious youth brands. In 2000 the Whitechapel Art Gallery in the East End of London, founded in 1901 to bring art to the working classes, put on an exhibition called *'Protest & Survive'*. It was named after an old anti-nuclear slogan. This was an exhibition of 'protest art'. This was not art that also had a political message; the art was created to convey a political message. The exhibits were polemical. The message of the exhibition was explicitly anti-capitalist and anti-corporate. Many of the more recent exhibits were manifestations of the art of anti-branding. A special walkway, apparently a work of art in itself and seemingly constructed out of old packing cases, had been built to connect the Whitechapel Art Gallery with the building, across an alleyway, of the anarchist Freedom Press and its bookshop.[24] This press is the publisher of the anarchist paper *Freedom* and was co-founded in 1886 by the revolutionary and leading anarchist of his generation and founder of anarcho-communism, Prince Peter Kropotkin.[25] The idea behind connecting the gallery with the anarchist bookshop was seemingly that once visitors had been to see some anti-capitalist art, they could buy some anti-capitalist theory, perhaps Kropotkin's own *Anarchism and Anarchist Communism* or his *Memoirs of a Revolutionist*. This exhibition was sponsored by Bloomberg,[26] the media company best known for its terminals providing stock prices to finance houses and brokers, and its 24 hour TV financial news channel. In 1998 Bloomberg had estimated revenues of $1.5 billion.[27] It has apparently made its founder and majority shareholder, Michael Bloomberg, a fortune of $4.5 billion.[28] He stepped down as Chief Executive of Bloomberg in order to run, as a Republican, for Mayor of New York, leading some to describe him as 'the new Citizen Kane'.[29] He was elected Mayor in November 2001, having spent $69 million, or $92.60 per vote, on his election campaign.[30] It must be somewhat galling for an anti-capitalist to go to an exhibition of anti-capitalist art, and then find that a multi-national corporation sponsors it. And not just any multi-national corporation but one that has developed a brand intimately connected with the very apotheosis of capitalism, indeed the engine rooms of globalisation, the financial markets. Even though he was a prince, Kropotkin must be turning in his grave at such a seemingly unsuitable marriage of revolutionary theory and corporate practice. It is little wonder that anti-capitalists see the warm embrace their icons have been subjected to from capitalists not only as a case of commercial exploitation but as a symptom of what Marxist theorist, and darling of 1960s radicals, Herbert Marcuse termed 'repressive tolerance'.

How else are anti-capitalists to explain a phenomenon which appears to be so at odds with their belief that capitalists only promote ideas which serve their own interests, or the wider interests of capitalists?

Corporations have appropriated the language and causes once associated with radical protest

From the activists' point of view, the use of anti-capitalist imagery by capitalist brands is bad enough. The appropriation of language, and thus the concepts this language underpins, is, however, even worse. It undermines the protesters 'ownership' of these concepts. Corporations have obviously not appropriated anti-capitalist rhetoric wholesale. Many corporations have, however, taken on board some of the concepts once associated with those who, at the very least, were highly critical of the workings of capitalism and modern corporations. A study of recent corporate mission statements and annual reports from major multinational corporations found many such documents with much to say about the corporation's commitment to the environment, equal opportunities, empowerment, good labour relations, reducing inequalities and being a force for change.[31] This is especially true of those corporations whose products are consumer brands. Therefore for anti-corporate activists simply to state that they are concerned about the environment, abhor bad labour practices, or are working for social change will not have much of an impact. For the corporations, especially those owning the most visible consumer brands, will turn around and state that they too are committed to social change, they too are concerned about the environment and improving the lot of workers in the South. What is more, they will say, this is what they have done about these issues. They have instituted an 'environmental policy' covering their manufacturing processes that goes further than that proposed by organisation x, some environmental NGO, and that this policy is independently audited. The labour practices of their sub-contractors in the South are also regularly subject to independent audits to see if they meet the standards proposed by organisation y, another NGO. To finally clinch the argument and prove the corporation's progressive credentials, they will point out that last year they gave z millions to such and such progressive causes. The types of donation usually mentioned in this context are, for example, the millions corporate

America gives to the NAACP,[32] the old established civil rights campaigners who were at the forefront of opposing segregation in the Southern states of the USA, the corporate support in the UK for Shelter,[33] the group which provides help to the homeless and seeks to keep the issue of homelessness in the public eye, or the $2.5 million Swedish furniture brand IKEA gave to map the world's disappearing forests after hearing about the project's lack of funding from Greenpeace International.[34]

The activists see this whole phenomenon as taking what they see as their own language, their own ideas, and their own organisations and then having these ideas used by what they see as the enemy, the multinational corporation. They believe that any organisation that receives corporate support must somehow have been domesticated in the interests of the status quo, the interests of multinational capitalism. Why else, they reason, would capitalists support a cause, if they were not using it to boost their own sales, or else had co-opted or neutered it in their own interests? The anti-branding campaigners believe the world is a place that is neatly divided between 'us' and 'them', 'exploited' and 'exploiter', 'people' and 'corporation'. The use by brands of the language, symbolism, and the concepts once associated with protest, obscures what the anti-branders see as a clear, objective, and insurmountable divide. This dichotomisation of the world into those, the many, who are innocent and are victims, and those, the few, who are guilty and are victimisers is, for the anti-branders, an absolute truth never to be questioned; it is their *sine qua non*.

When anti-capitalist claims prove false, new claims - such as those about branding - are constructed

It used to be an easier task for the radicals to portray the world as neatly dichotomised, and to persuade others to believe it as well. Things seemed neater then. This is not primarily because corporations were less prone to express, for example, environmental concerns in days gone by. More central is the changing imagery of advertising. In the past corporate advertising never used gay imagery, portrayed women as doing the housework and children as being obedient, and rarely showed blacks or Asians and when they did they were often in menial or stereotypical roles. The 1960s generation of anti-capitalists argued that these groups were portrayed as such, because the capitalists needed to maintain, indeed even construct, patriarchal models of the family and racist attitudes in order to sustain their profits, and thus to sustain capitalism itself. Capitalists used advertising, so the argument went, to inculcate the assumptions and values associated with patriarchy and racism.

The 1960s critics of capitalism believed that by challenging racism, traditional gender roles, and conventional sexual behaviour, they were somehow challenging capitalism itself. Imagine the shock of the activists when they saw advertising that celebrated black empowerment, put powerful and independent women on a pedestal, and portrayed homosexuality as chic. This was not meant to happen. Did capitalism not need these traditional notions to survive and had they not learnt that challenging these notions would fatally undermine capitalism? Were not these traditional notions one of the great, and inevitable, evils of capitalism?

One might have thought that they would have acknowledged the fact that their arguments had been proved wrong, and questioned the underlying assumptions of anti-capitalism. This has not, however, happened. The critics of capitalism have responded to the manifest errors of their earlier arguments in their usual manner. In this case as in so many others, when the old reasons for hating capitalism have proved quite simply to be false, new reasons for hating it have been found. As the pre-eminent historian of economic thought, Professor Mark Blaug puts it when describing Marxism: 'What a wonderful story is the history of Marxism, refuted again and again, and revised again and again - not by its enemies but by its friends.'[35] This applies just as much to anti-capitalism in its other guises.

The lessons from the failures of the anti-capitalists' earlier claims: advertising is responsive to changing social attitudes
If the anti-capitalists had considered the proven failure of their earlier claims, they could have drawn certain conclusions. For the changing images found in advertising surely show three things. The first is how responsive advertising is to changes in social attitudes. The changing representation of women, gays, and blacks and Asians in advertising is a reflection of the changing attitudes in society as a whole. In other words corporations, individually or collectively, cannot simply impose a world view upon society through advertising.

Corporations are an integral part of society, not separate from it

The second is that the corporations are not separate from society; they are an integral part of it. Wider social change is also occurring within the corporation. Indeed, the authoritative British Social Attitudes study shows that liberal attitudes on issues such as homosexuality, gender roles, and immigration are much more widespread, and indeed more deeply held, among the professional and managerial classes, ie, those who are the managers and executives in the large corporations, than they are in society as a whole.[36] Similar patterns are discernible in the USA, perhaps to an even greater extent. In a recent highly acclaimed, and amusing, book, *Bobos in Paradise: The New Upper Class and How They Got There*,[37] David Brooks argues that liberal social attitudes have become the dominant values of the professional and managerial elite, and celebrates this fact. Many of those at the top of large corporations have been marked by the student radicalism of the 1960s, either directly or, for those younger, by the social changes this brought about. While the anti-capitalist ethos of student protest has largely been abandoned by this generation as they have grown up, they have widely retained their liberal social attitudes and have become bourgeois bohemians. This is an ethos which is widely shared by their younger successors.

Anti-capitalist claims about the nature of capitalism say much about the prejudices of anti-capitalists, but nothing about the nature of capitalism

The third relates to the nature of the earlier charge itself. Claims are so often made by anti-capitalists in relation to all manner of phenomena they happen to disapprove of, that such and such is occurring, or such and such attitudes are prevalent, or society is structured in such and such a way, because capitalism needs it to be. Such claims have again and again been shown to be wholly unfounded. The structures or attitudes attacked have changed, indeed often been utterly transformed, yet the market system has not fallen. Something that has little or nothing to do with the market system *per se*, such as images of traditional gender roles in advertising, is conjoined with it. This is simply because those doing the conjoining disapprove not only of capitalism but also of traditional gender roles, or whatever else might be their particular *bête noire.* Anything that bad, the reasoning seems to go, must be a product of capitalism. Then some dubious rationale is found for this conjoining. Such arguments tell us more about the attitudes of the anti-capitalists than about the phenomenon they are trying to explain. Since it has so often been proved to be false, it must surely be overdue for anti-capitalists to abandon this type of argument.

The errors of the earlier claims about advertising have not, however, caused the anti-capitalists to re-evaluate their antipathy towards capitalism. The anti-capitalists have simply found a new reason for hating the market without truly acknowledging the errors of their earlier claims. A new rationale has had to be constructed which, in the activists' minds, once again divides the world into the innocent many and the guilty few. Anti-branding, and the current attacks on corporations for using progressive ideas, imagery and language, is one such rationale. The activists can sleep happy in the knowledge that all is as it should be. The world is thus, after all, still neatly divided and they can still see themselves as being partisans for altruism over rapacious capitalist greed, and as fighters for 'the people' against the privilege that they believe the few have gained at the expense of the many. The anti-branders see it as their role to make this perception of a dichotomised world, which is so self-evident and glaring to them, apparent to all. It never occurs to the anti-branders to question the correctness of this position.

Re-constructing the divide: what the anti-branding movement is trying to achieve

The purpose of the anti-branding movement is to make other people see the world in the same way the anti-branders see it and thus to sell an idea, namely that corporations are the problem and can never be part of the solution. As the leading anti-brander Tim O'Connor of Nikewatch puts it, 'Nike has been a useful target to make a wider point about globalization'.[38] These activists have joined the branding business, except in their case it is the negative branding of the corporations which they believe are selling the public a lie. The anti-branders seek to project their message by highlighting, through the use of powerful and arresting imagery, alleged abuses by the corporations which own consumer brands.

The tarnishing of the reputation, the damaging of the brand, is the primary purpose here; the actual specific charge, whether it is about employment practices, the environment, or where a company buys its raw materials, is secondary. The anti-branding campaigners are not seeking simply to get a corporation to pay its employees slightly more or to change this or that specific environmental practice. The damage to the brand's reputation is the aim. Or more precisely it is the immediate aim, with the hope that the tarnishing of what the activists view as the widely perceived human face of capitalism - namely consumer brands, especially those brands which portray themselves as being progressive - will tarnish the reputation of capitalism as a whole.

This is why brands that seek to adopt a progressive image are targeted especially. Klein puts it succinctly: 'We have heard the refrain over and over again from Nike, Reebok, The Body Shop, Starbucks, Levi's, and The Gap: "Why are you picking on us? We're the good ones!" The answer is simple. They are singled out because the politics they have associated themselves with, which have made them rich - feminism, ecology, inner-city empowerment - were not just random pieces of effective ad copy that their brand mangers found lying around. They are complex, essential social ideas, for which many people have spent lifetimes fighting. That's what lends righteousness to the rage of activists campaigning against what they see as cynical distortions of those ideas.'[39] In other words these brands are attacked because they portray themselves as being progressive, because they proclaim their belief in corporate social responsibility, not in spite of it.

'Progressive' brands are easier to attack

The fact that these brands portray themselves as being progressive also makes it easier to attack them for practical reasons. As Klein goes on to say, 'companies such as Levi's and The Body Shop can't shrug them [calls for corporate social accountability] off, because they publicly presented social accountability as the foundation of their corporate philosophy from the first. Over and over again, it is when the advertising teams creatively overreach themselves that - like Icarus - they fall.'[40]

When brands institute an environmental or a human rights policy or code of conduct, especially of the precise and rigorous sort favoured by many of the brands Klein highlights, it will be very likely that campaigners will be able to find some alleged infringement of this code. The activists will look for some action by some supplier or some subsidiary, which appears to infringe this code, or can be portrayed as infringing it.

It is highly likely that the activists will be able to find something to fit their requirements when dealing with a large and diffuse corporation spread across various continents. Large multi-national corporations will inevitably have difficulty in uniformly implementing such a code, and even greater difficulty in imposing its code upon suppliers. Since many such codes specifically deal with, and were in fact set up to deal with, the employment practices of suppliers, often smallish scale producers on the opposite side of the world from where the code has been drawn up, this is usually where such breaches are to be found. Through the adoption of such codes, the brands have set themselves a benchmark against which they can be tested. And, not surprisingly, they are. If the brands appear to fall below the benchmarks they have set themselves, they can be attacked for this far more clearly than if this benchmark had never existed. The anti-branders can then claim that such codes are worthless; they concentrate on the few cases where they can show the company's code has been infringed and ignore the vast number of cases where the company's code has been adhered to.

By simply hyping alleged infringements, the anti-branders ignore the very real impact such codes can and do have on how companies operate and the very real benefits such codes, if carefully and thoughtfully devised and implemented, can and indeed have produced for the environment and the people they are seeking to protect. The tarring of the corporate reputation is the anti-branders aim, and corporate codes can be an aid in this exercise. Here again, as in so much else, the activists perceive a world in which everything is not perfect as one in which everything is imperfect; they construct an all or nothing world for themselves.

Anti-branding as marketing - 'It's a gateway drug'

The anti-brand movement has learnt to employ, at a fraction of the brander's costs, the brander's techniques and, just like the brands, it too has a product to sell. Anti-branding is an attempt to market a carefully defined product, in this case anti-corporate ideas and sentiment and more specifically the notion of a dichotomised world, in an easily digestible form. How does the activist get this idea across to young people who are not especially interested in politics (for which the activist will obviously blame the machinations of the brands and corporations in general) and who do not feel particularly victimised themselves (again the machinations of the brands in constructing false ideas of contentment)? A picture of a dreadful looking factory in the South, where Brand X allegedly manufacture their products, is far more effective than trying to discuss with them the nature of wage labour, perhaps illustrated - if this particular activist is of Marxist bent - by reference to 'the industrial reserve army' and the 'impoverishment thesis' and quotes from Section 3 of chapter 25, vol.1 of *Das Kapital*.[41] All the better if Brand X thus attacked is one which appeals to youth. It is surely no accident, to use that old chestnut of the left, that the brands most attacked by the anti-brand activists - those mentioned by Klein above - are precisely those products which appeal to a youth market, ie, precisely the market to which the anti-brand activists are trying to appeal.

Klein, arguing in *The Guardian* that in the wake of the September 11th terrorist attacks on New York and Washington DC the anti-corporate movement is more relevant than ever, quotes a fellow activist approvingly when she says that Nike was never the target of her activism but merely a tool to get her message across. 'It's a gateway drug'. Klein goes on to say 'For years, we in the movement have fed off our opponents' symbols - their brands, their office towers, their photo-opportunity summits. We have used them as rallying cries, as focal points, as popular education tools. But these symbols were never the real targets: they were the levers, the handles.'[42] In other words, what Klein is acknowledging is that anti-branding is a marketing device.

What remains of organised Marxist-Leninism in the UK, the Trotskyist organisations and their papers such as the *Socialist Worker* and *Workers Power*, have become aware of the utility of anti-branding as a device for selling their ideology. These groups now repeatedly use attacks on brands in their papers and their propaganda.[43] Theirs is a fairly recent interest in anti-branding, which has developed since they have seen the success of the broader anti-branding movement.

London Greenpeace and McLibel: a classic example of anti-branding activism

To illustrate these points, it is worth examining the activities of

London Greenpeace, also known by the name of their web site McSpotlight. This organisation describes itself as 'an open, anarchist, ecological group which has always supported a wide range of radical, social, and environmental issues, networking with other activists and initiatives.'[44] This organisation, which has no connection with Greenpeace International, runs a major anti-brand web site and came to public prominence over the so-called McLibel case. This court case, and London Greepeace's actions which led to it, were the defining moment of the anti-branding movement in the UK, and what really launched it into the public vision.

Two London Greenpeace activists, the so-called 'McLibel Two' - David Steel and Helen Morris - were sued for libel by McDonald's for producing and distributing leaflets attacking McDonald's. After 313 days of evidence and legal argument, and England's longest ever trial, on 19th June 1997 Mr Justice Bell in the High Court, unusually in a case for libel sitting without a jury because of its length and complexity, found unequivocally for McDonald's, awarding damages of £60,000.[45] In spite of this, the fact that Mr Justice Bell did not reject all the disputed claims made in the leaflet has subsequently been used by opponents of McDonald's to muddy the waters as to the outcome of the case.

McDonald's won the legal battle, but lost the public relations war

Whilst McDonald's were the victors legally, they undoubtedly lost the public relations battle. The so-called 'McLibel Two' managed to turn the action against them into a trial of McDonald's. Their erroneous accusations against McDonald's thus received much more coverage than the original leaflets would ever have done. The publicity the case generated, and the ease with which protest leaflets can be distributed and printed off via the Internet, made the London Greenpeace leaflets, in their own words, 'probably the most famous and widely distributed protest leaflets in history'.[46]

Immeasurable numbers have viewed these leaflets on the net, three million hard copies have apparently been distributed in the UK since the point when McDonald's started its action and the leaflets have been translated into at least 26 languages.[47] Even though the judge found that the 'McLibel Two' had committed 'serious and important libels'[48] and awarded damages to

McDonald's, the 'McLibel Two' can claim 'we have recently emerged victorious from a huge legal and public battle against McDonald's, another high profile global company making strenuous efforts to project a benevolent image'.[49] They believe themselves to be victorious because of the damage they correctly believe they have inflicted upon the reputation of McDonald's. As David Hooper, a lawyer and leading commentator on British libel cases puts it, 'The publicity thus given to the views of the defendants must have exceeded McDonald's worst nightmares. Certainly it must have dented any promotion the company's annual advertising budget of $2 billion could have bought.'[50]

The McLibel case is the classic example of anti-branding activism. As John Vidal, *Guardian* journalist and the author of a book about the case highly sympathetic to the 'McLibel Two', puts it, 'McLibel is a battle of image, an appeal by both sides for the hearts and minds of the public'.[51] It is not about 'shaming' a corporation into changing this or that practice, using this kind of packaging instead of that kind. It is about damaging a corporation's reputation. By damaging that corporation's reputation they aim not only to damage that corporation's reputation, but also to damage the reputation of all corporations - or at least, for the less doctrinaire anti-branders, all but the very smallest corporations - and thus the reputation of capitalism.

Somewhat ironically for two anarchists who claim to be passionately opposed to the whole notion of leaders, David Steel and Helen Morris have been eulogised by the anti-branding movement for their 'struggle' against McDonald's. Every recent anti-corporate book seems to devote space to their 'brave and heroic fight'. They are portrayed as role models and groups around the world carefully study their tactics. Channel 4 has even made a TV dramatisation of their court case. This can only be described as a massive marketing achievement for what was a small, fairly obscure, near zero budget, doctrinaire activist group. They would not have received even a fraction of this coverage, or the widespread mainstream sympathy and support they have, if they had only produced pamphlets espousing their ideology of green anarchism and had not gone into the anti-branding business. Anti-branding has meant that two activists who are indubitably on the farthest fringes of UK politics have received sympathy even from Middle England. Projecting their campaign as a David and Goliath battle between two plucky individuals and the might of a multi-national corporation is bound to elicit sympathy.

The McLibel campaigners move on to attack The Body Shop
Interestingly, the other 'high profile global company making strenuous efforts to project a benevolent image' compared to McDonald's in the quote above is that quintessential 'ethical consumer' brand, The Body Shop. The 'McLibel Two' and London Greenpeace are targeting this brand because they want to reach the kind of people who are attracted to The Body Shop. London Greenpeace are in battle for hearts and minds and their target is the whole notion of 'ethical consumerism'. They are trying to persuade those who are attracted to 'ethical consumerism' that there is no such thing. The Body Shop is a brand whose 'ethical' message is not a bonus to its customers, but is central to its appeal, makes a great deal of its support for environmental causes,[52] and whose co-founder, Anita Roddick, is probably the face of 'ethical' consumerism. London Greenpeace's message is well illustrated in their hostile remarks about The Body Shop. They wrote that: 'The Body Shop have over 1,500 stores in 47 countries, and aggressive expansion plans'. They go on to assume that The Body Shop's purpose, like that of all multi-nationals, is to make lots of money for their shareholders, whom they again assume to be rich. They assert, more or less as an article of faith, that The Body Shop is driven by power and greed. Since The Body Shop is obviously in disagreement with this, they accuse The Body Shop of somehow concealing its true nature. Such claims tell us nothing about The Body Shop but much about the prejudices of theses activists. Such claims are made to reinforce London Greenpeace's central contention, namely that 'The truth is that nobody can make the world a better place by shopping.'[53]

By attacking The Body Shop, London Greenpeace is trying to get across the notion of a dichotomised world, a world divided between the exploited 'us' of the people, and the exploiting 'them' of the corporation. By attacking The Body Shop they are showing that their issue is capitalism itself. 'Our basic point is to demonstrate that the problem is not this or that particular company, but the economic system based on profits and power'.[54] This is the rationale of all of London Greenpeace's campaigns, and indeed of all of the campaigns of anti-branders in general. Whether they are against Nike, McDonald's or The Body Shop is immaterial. The point of these campaigns is not to persuade a given corporation to change a given practice or withdraw from a given activity. Yet again their point is to sell the anti-branders' underlying message about a mutually hostile, dichotomised world.

3

The Complex Web of Consumers, Owners, and Funders

The myth of a dichotomised world: the power of the consumer

In fact the world is much more complex than the anti-branders' world view allows for. There is no neat divide between them and us. Who has made the brands what they are today? It is the individual choices of millions of consumers. Coca-Cola, McDonald's and Nike have not become powerful brands due to some sinister conspiracy. These brands are what they are, because millions of consumers enjoy consuming their products, and prefer their products to those of their competitors.

The anti-branders are, of course, aware of this and seeking to overcome this obstacle is in many ways the *raison d'être* of the anti-branding argument. It is the reason for the endless desire by anti-corporate activists to somehow show that the consumers' choices do not reflect their true desires, their true interests. The anti-branders regard the modern high street, with its preponderance of branded shops and large impersonal chain stores as malign. They cannot bear the notion that this type of high street has arisen because of consumer choice, that consumers as a group have shown their preference for McDonald's and Sainsbury's over the pie and mash shop or the local green grocer. The anti-branders thus construct an argument that shifts blame back from the consumer to the corporations, from the many to the few.

The ownership base of major corporations has become very broad

The second complication is that the ownership of the corporations is no longer the reserve of a select, privileged few. At the end of 2000, institutional investors owned 47.1 per cent of UK shares, with a combined value of £855 billion.[55] The largest constituents within this category were insurance companies, with holdings of £380.9 billion, or 21 per cent of UK shares, and pension funds, with £321.2 billion, or 17.7 per cent.[56] These holdings represent the collective savings of tens of millions; they will help pay for more comfortable retirements for tens of millions. Furthermore, non-UK investors owned 32.4 per cent of British shares.[57] Much of these overseas-owned equities represent the holdings of foreign - European, American, Japanese - pension funds and other collective investments that are not represented in the figures for UK institutional ownership and are in addition to them. In other words, the major corporations are in general today not owned by the few, but for the benefit of the many.

This represents a vast shift, and massive broadening, of corporate ownership: in 1963 institutional investors represented 29 per cent of UK shares, with pension funds representing only 6.4 per cent. Individuals then represented 54 per cent of shareholdings, now they represent 16 per cent.[58] Within the category of individual share-holders there has also been a huge broadening of ownership. Today there are an estimated 11·5 million private investors in the UK.[59] In the USA, 45 million people, or half the full-time private workforce, have 401K accounts. These enable workers tax efficiently to invest a percentage of their salary in the stock market.[60] These figures paint an altogether different picture from the activists' vision of a dichotomised world.

There is a third complication. Although it cannot be said to be as socially significant as the broadening of wealth and ownership has been, it is perhaps even more subversive of the anti-branders' perceptions to examine who supports and funds their anti-corporate, anti-branding campaigns.

The funding of anti-capitalism by capitalists - anti-branding funded by brand-created wealth

What if the campaigns the anti-branders are themselves engaged in are funded by the exploiting few of their own imagination? What if they are funded not just by any exploiting few, but by those who suggest, much to the fury of the anti-branders, that you can make the world a better place by shopping, indeed that corporations, specifically their corporations, are your friend? Here one is not considering support for those 'domesticated' issues and campaigns that the activists argue have been stolen from them by corporations in order to sell this year's trainers, etc. Nor is one talking of such somewhat cheeky, oh so daring, stunts as the anarchist band Chumbawamba donating the £70,000 fee they received for one of their songs to be used in a General Motors advertisement to the radical anti-branding, anti-corporate organisations, CorpWatch and IndyMedia.[61] The fact is that radical, indubitably undomesticated, anti-corporate activist groups, with a similar outlook to the organisations Chumbawamba gave money to, are the recipients of intentional funding by some brands, by individuals who have become extremely wealthy via brands, and by foundations endowed by those individuals. Such funding even extends to organisations whose sole purpose is to push forward the whole anti-branding agenda. Should this not make the activists question at least some of their assumptions? At the very least they should abandon their belief that any organisation that has ever received any funding from a corporation somehow becomes little more than a corporate stooge.

Brand-created wealth supports the anti-corporate training camps of the Ruckus Society

The Ruckus Society is a US organisation which holds training camps for anti-corporate activists in non-violent direct action. On its web site, the Ruckus Society asks 'are you sick of a corporate global economy that puts profits ahead of the environment, democracy, workers, human rights, justice and local communi- ties?'[62] It is described by the radical Anglo-American journalist Alexander Cockburn as one of 'the true heroes of the Battle of Seattle',[63] ie, the demonstrations in Seattle against the World Trade Organization's summit there in late November and early December 1999 which have become one of the defining moments of the new anti-corporate movement.

Alexander Cockburn contrasts the boisterous militants of the Ruckus Society, his heroes, with the liberal demonstrators such as those from the trade unions, mainstream environmental groups or those who might believe in 'ethical consumerism'. He denigrates the latter for being feeble, and too circumscribed in their actions by what Cockburn regards as a somewhat quaint desire not to upset people and to cultivate a responsible 'mainstream' image. This is something the Ruckus Society can never be accused of. During US universities' spring break it organises a Ruckus Society Spank the Bank Action Camp to train student radicals to 'confront the world's most destructive financial institution - the Citigroup'.[64] As the Society puts it, 'Ruckus trains and assists activists to use direct action to stop industries' relentless assault on the planet'.[65]

To sum up, the Ruckus Society is not an organisation which seeks to change this or that corporate practice or ameliorate one or other aspect of capitalism as it is found today. It seeks the radical transformation of society along fundamentally different principles.

How might an organisation such as this be funded? The Ruckus Society has taken on board one of the favourite fund-raising tools for myriad arts, conservationist and development causes. Many such organisations offer those who are so inclined the chance to sponsor a seat in the opera, a tree in an old forest, or a child in the South. The Ruckus Society offers the opportunity of sponsoring an activist. If you feel guilty about your corporate job, but do not feel like throwing it in to join the direct action brigade yourself, you can sponsor an activist to go to a Ruckus training camp for $400 and enjoy the pleasures of activism vicariously.

But, just as in the case of more mainstream organisations, this only raises a certain amount of money. Arts, conservation and development charities raise larger amounts of money via substantial donations from the extremely wealthy and the foundations which the extremely wealthy have established, and also from corporate support, often via corporate foundations. The Ruckus Society has also learnt from this and engages in such methods of fund-raising. Billionaire media mogul Ted Turner's foundation gave a $50,000 grant to the Ruckus Society in 1999, along with donations to myriad other progressive causes.[66]

Anita Roddick, who stepped down from a day-to-day role in The Body Shop in 2002 but remains a non-executive Director and 'creative consultant'[67], is listed as a Director of the Ruckus Society.[68] The Body Shop Foundation gave the Ruckus Society a $40,000 grant in 2000 towards its training camps.[69] The Ruckus Society, along with Naomi Klein, has contributed to a book edited by Anita Roddick, *Take It Personally - How Globalization Affects You and How to Fight Back*.[70] It is a glossy, coffee table guide, full of arresting images and pictures, aimed at the uninitiated on how to get involved in the burgeoning protest movement, and why you should. Those buying this book can rest assured that proceeds 'are going to support visionaries, grassroots groups, and non-governmental organisations who are debunking the myths created by the World

Trade Organization.'[71] Anita Roddick and her husband, Gordon Roddick, are so committed to these campaigns that they have pledged to leave all their money to The Body Shop Foundation to fund progressive causes, not leaving their children 'anything beyond a trust fund and the houses we own'.[72]

The TV stations of Turner and the skin care products and lotions of the Roddicks are, of course, themselves identified by the anti-branders with all the alleged sins of branding. They are, in fact, seen as especially heinous offenders by some: the mainstream media represented by Ted Turner is seen as the engine behind the construction of the branded world and Anita Roddick is the champion of what they see as the blind alley of 'ethical consumerism'. Hence, The Body Shop was a prominent target on the web-based hit list of corporations to be subject to 'anti-capitalist actions on Tuesday 1st May 2001'.[73] These actions were planned as part of a global day of anti-corporate protest of which the Ruckus Society was very much an element. In the end no actual actions took place against The Body Shop due to robust policing and the shops in the vicinity of the main anti-capitalist march taking extensive precautions such as boarding up their windows etc. In the cases of Ted Turner and The Body Shop, however, the support given to the Ruckus Society is not via their corporations, although The Body Shop Foundation is manifestly and intimately identified with The Body Shop, and is given much exposure on The Body Shop web site.

Patagonia, a brand of hiking and sports clothing, makes much of its environmental ideals. As part of this commitment it gives 10 per cent of its pre-tax profits to 'grass root environmental organisations'. One of the organisations Patagonia boasts of supporting on its web site, with a grant of $30,000, is the Ruckus Society.[74] Furthermore, Patagonia offers to post bail for Ruckus protesters arrested for non-violent direct action.[75]

Unilever's indirect donations to anti-corporate organisations
Ben & Jerry ice-cream is another famous 'ethical' brand. Its founders, Ben Cohen and Jerry Greenfield, committed the company to donate 7.5 per cent of its pre-tax profits to not-for-profit organisations, partly to 'grassroots organisations throughout the United States which facilitate progressive social change' via the Ben & Jerry Foundation.[76] When the founders sold out to global consumer brand conglomerate Unilever for $326 million in 2000,

Unilever committed itself to continue supporting the Ben & Jerry Foundation to the tune of at least $1.1 million per year for at least 10 years,[77] and on top of this gave the foundation a one-off $5 million at the time of the take-over.[78] In 2001, ie, after the take-over by Unilever, the Ben & Jerry Foundation, amongst donations to other progressive organisations, gave $100,000 to the Ruckus Society,[79] a $15,000 grant to Sweatshop Watch to further its work and a $10,000 to the Institute for Social Ecology for its work in organising and educating networks of anti-biotech activists.[80]

Sweatshop Watch is at the forefront of targeting clothing brands for their, and their sub-contractors, employment practices. A favourite device it employs is comparing the lowly pay received by those producing goods in the South with high executive pay in the North. Ironically, the Chief Executive of Unilever, Niall Fitzgerald is not only one of the most vocal defenders of globalisation in corporate Britain[81] but is also one of the highest paid 'bosses' in the UK, being paid £1.3 million in 2000.[82]

The Institute for Social Ecology is one of green anarchist Murray Bookchin's organisations.[83] He is a leading anti-capitalist thinker, and a guru for many of the more radical of today's protesters, including London Greenpeace and the McLibel Two. Bookchin is the founder of the credo of social ecology and a prolific author both of books postulating a green anarchist society and tracts excoriating other greens and assorted radicals for what he perceives as the errors of their analysis and their compromises. His books include *'Post-Scarcity Anarchism', 'Anarchism, Marxism and the Future of the Left', 'Which Way for the Ecology Movement'* and the three volume *'The Third Revolution'*. Bookchin's notion of social ecology differentiates itself from other radical green thought by seeing itself as part of a left-wing revolutionary tradition, seeing environment-alism as only one part of a wider anti-capitalist message, and exclusively blaming capitalism in general and corporations in particular for environmental degradation (as opposed to human activity as a whole).[84] Murray Bookchin is admired among the anti-branders for the purity of his vision and his complete unwillingness to make any compromises with capitalism. For many of today's anti-branders Bookchin's ideas are the theoretical underpinning for their actions. They see Bookchin as offering a truly revolutionary, virulently anti-capitalist ideology, untainted by the failures of Marxism. Yet as this funding shows, however indirectly, even

Bookchin has received financial support from a multi-national, indeed from one of the major global purveyors of branded goods.

The Foundation for Deep Ecology: brand-created wealth funds anti-corporate, anti-branding groups such as Adbusters

Perhaps the most well established anti-branding organisation is the Canadian-based Adbusters Foundation, which has made an international name for itself. This is well-deserved because, whatever one may think of the validity of their explicitly anti-consumerist message, they produce many genuinely witty and clever parodies of real advertisements and carry out amusing stunts. These are disseminated via the Internet and also through their well-produced glossy magazine, *Adbusters - The Journal of the Mental Environment*. Where one would expect to find advertisements in such a magazine, one finds parodies of advertisements.

Adbusters is so renowned for the cleverness of its advertisment parodies that they even offer, via something called the Powershift Advocacy Agency, their skills 'in helping other organisations deliver the messages the world needs to hear . . . if your communications are not-for-profit, consider Powershift when you call agencies. We're a full-service shop, ready to create your next campaign - if the cause is right.'[85] Adbusters also try to buy TV time for their anti-consumerist advertisements, which the networks usually refuse.[86] Obviously the networks' refusal to air these advertisements gives Adbusters a propaganda coup.

The founder of Adbusters, Kalle Lasn is the author of another, more specifically American, best-selling manifesto and history of the anti-branding movement, *Culture Jam - How to Reverse America's Suicidal Consumer Binge - And Why We Must*.[87] Yet Adbusters have received funding from wealth created through American consumer brands during America's alleged 'consumer binge'.

Adbusters' publications have received support from the $170 million Foundation for Deep Ecology.[88] This foundation, which has awarded grants of over $50 million to 'the boldest, most visionary [activist] groups working to . . . fight megatechnology and industrial globalization'[89] between 1990 and 2001, was established by Doug Tompkins, when he sold Esprit, the hugely successful clothing brand he had founded. Alongside the Foundation for Deep

Ecology, he founded a wholly separate foundation to buy up and protect wilderness in South America. The foundation has bought up 800,000 acres of temperate rainforest in Chile, at a cost of $10 million, to establish the Pumalin Park nature reserve, and a foundation set up by Doug Tomkins' wife, Kris McDivitt - the founder of aforementioned Patagonia clothing brand - has bought up a further 260,000 acres of Argentina. In total this couple and their foundations' own more than two million acres of Chile and Argentina.[90]

These efforts have been heavily criticised in South America for restricting development in these areas. Since restrictions on development are the point of such nature reserves, this must be regarded as a success within their own remit. Ironically, considering the Foundation for Deep Ecology's support for anti-capitalist organisations, these foundations are an excellent example of the effectiveness of private property rights based conservation efforts. It shows how wilderness, habitats, or whatever else a given group of people hold dear, can be protected from development within the framework of capitalism.

Founding Esprit would be a serious enough offence in the anti-branders eyes, but Doug Tompkins is a recidivist. He founded not just Esprit, but an equally successful, youth-oriented consumer brand in the shape of the trendy outdoor clothing label, The North Face. Esprit and The North Face are exactly the kind of brands most attacked by the anti-branders. According to their detractors, they sought a progressive, rebellious, friendly image whilst behaving just like any other large corporation Indeed Naomi Klein apparently first discovered the evils of brands and global corporations when she was sacked, aged 17, from a part-time job in Esprit for displaying a 'bad attitude' while being told that Esprit was her 'good friend'.[91]

Alexander Cockburn ridicules Doug Tompkins as 'the former czar of sweatshop-made sports clothing who funds the [highly anti-globalisation, for its alleged worsening of labour conditions and impact upon the environment] International Forum on Globalization.'[92] For Cockburn, Tompkins and his ilk are not the true face of protest; they are not radical enough for Cockburn's tastes and are perceived by him to be somewhat hypocritical. Yet their munificence is no small part of the reason why the radical anti-corporate, anti-branding movement favoured by Cockburn has become what it is today.

It is ironic that the anti-corporate movement's financial fortunes are intimately tied up with the fortunes of the capitalist economy. The movement has relied on funding from foundations and others whose coffers swelled during the economic and share price boom; in a recession and with falling share prices their coffers shrink. James Harding of the *Financial Times* notes that, 'September 11th threatens to provide an ugly illustration of how tightly the movement has become tied to the mainstream economy . . . activism prospered on the back of America's boom, the movement now promises to suffer financially as the West teeters towards recession.'[93]

The sources of funding for anti-corporate campaigns should make activists question their assumptions

The fact that the anti-corporate movement is reliant upon capitalist wealth to fund its campaigns undermines its vision of the world as neatly divided between the exploiting few and the exploited many. This caricatured view has perhaps found its apotheosis in the UK in the writings of anti-corporate author and *Guardian* columnist George Monbiot. As *Independent* journalist David Aaronovitch, himself once rather left-wing, puts it, 'Monbiot's view of life is underwritten by a Socialist Sunday School notion of how capitalism works... This is too simple, even for Harry Potter . . . What grates is his patronising and simplistic way of writing. Protesters are all poor ordinary folk... Their opponents are ... "rotund" and "ponderous". So this becomes a bipolar, almost visual, fight between people and business - like Hollywood.'[94]

Not only are capitalists invariably up to all types of wickedness in his column, he is also permanently on the look out for greens and anti-corporate types in general who appear to have betrayed the true faith. Monbiot has strongly attacked the former head of Greenpeace UK (the British affiliate of Greenpeace International), Lord Peter Melchett, for taking a job with corporate PR company Burson Marsteller. In *The Guardian*, Monbiot accuses Lord Melchett of succumbing to his class interest, 'Rich and powerful greens must perpetually contest their class interest. Environmentalism, just as much as socialism, involves the restraint of wealth and power. Peter Melchett, like Tolstoy, Kropotkin, Engels, Orwell, and Tony Benn, was engaged in counter-identity politics.'[95]

What Monbiot is saying is that these people, from privileged backgrounds - and by implication Monbiot himself who also comes from a privileged background - were acting against what Monbiot perceives as their own class interest. This language seeks to reinforce the dichotomised world view so beloved of the radical activists. Such criticisms of Melchett, however, are easy for radical activists to make. They can hold on to their cosy assumptions and forget how reliant their campaigns are upon corporate and corporate-created wealth. This is not wealth which has been inherited through the generations, as in Monbiot's examples, but wealth directly created by the active corporate capitalism of the donors. Monbiot goes on to say: 'Environmentalism, like almost everything else, is in danger of being swallowed up by the corporate leviathan. If this happens, it will disappear without trace. No one threatens its survival as much as the greens who have taken the company shilling'.[96]

His prediction that taking corporate money will destroy the green movement is clearly wrong. The green movement is awash with corporate, and corporate-created, money, yet has certainly not disappeared. Anti-corporate, anti-consumerist activism does not lose its ferocity because it is in receipt of corporate funds. The statement says more about the wish of radical activists for a neatly dichotomised world than about the reality of the situation.

George Monbiot and his fellow activists should consider where some of the money behind the anti-corporate, anti-consumerist campaigns originates. They should also consider how broad the ownership of the corporations, and thus those who profit from them, has become. They might then think twice before yet again reiterating their belief in the existence of a clear, unambiguous and universal divide between the 'us' of 'the people' and the protesters, and the 'them' of the corporations and the wealthy. Perhaps they would then begin to realise that the world is rather more complex, and perhaps more schizophrenic, than the projection they put upon it allows for. They would have to stop believing that the corporate world is somehow a monolith. They would also have to reconsider their belief in the growing menace of corporate censorship.

A media mogul in the shape of Ted Turner, the founder of one of the world's most influential news organisations CNN, giving money to this movement squares ill with their belief that the movement is excluded by the mainstream media. There is, however, no evidence that such a reconsideration is occurring among the protesters. The belief in a neatly dichotomised world is too comfortable and useful a construct for the protestors to discard even when the reality of their own campaigns so clearly shows up its vacuity.

4

Motives Old and New: Companies as Targets for Protest

Not all attacks on corporations are motivated by the ideology of anti-branding

The targeting of The Body Shop and Nike shows that any corporation, regardless of how hard it tries to project a 'caring' and 'concerned' image, can be subject to attacks and campaigns against it by the anti-brand activists. Indeed corporations are especially vulnerable to such campaigns if they seek to project such an image. Getting into bed with the campaigners will not stop a brand from being targeted by those whose central preoccupation is a fundamental and ideological opposition to consumerism and corporations.

However not all attacks on brands are motivated by anti-branding and its ancillary ideologies. Attacks upon brands are also motivated by three other broad categories of reason. The divide between these categories is not, however, a clean one. There is a certain overlap between these categories, and also between them and anti-branding.

Campaigners who want to change a specific corporate policy

Many campaigners are genuinely interested in changing this or that policy of this or that corporation, and see the boycotting and pillorying of specific corporations as a way of achieving this. A good example of this kind of activism is the originally US-based, Internet-led, campaign to stop Western corporations from investing in Burma. Those behind this campaign are concerned with the Burmese government's appalling human rights record and suppression of democracy, and believe that foreign investment will shore up the regime. The campaign has been highly successful in persuading Western consumer brands not to use, or to cease using, suppliers and sub-contractors in Burma, and also to stop them from marketing their products in Burma. This campaign has persuaded, amongst others, Levi Strauss, Macy's Department Stores, Liz Claiborne, British Home Stores, Heineken, Carlsberg, and Pepsi, after losing a $1 million contract with Harvard University as a result of the campaign, to disengage from Burma.[97] The campaign has even persuaded, after they were threatened with a consumer boycott, major Californian wine producers to stop marketing their wines to Burma.

Consumer brands are, obviously, those most easily subject to consumer boycotts, so tend to be the obvious and most effective targets of such campaigns. Interestingly these campaigns about Burma have been very significantly helped by that bogeyman of anti-globalisers of both left and right, billionaire financier and prodigious philanthropist George Soros and his laudable Open Society Fund. The Fund, more widely associated with Eastern Europe and the former Soviet Union, seeks to help build the institutions of civil society and create the right conditions for democracy and the rule of law to flourish. It has a special Burma Project which is the leading source of information on Burma, its human rights situation and, from a critical perspective, on those companies investing there.[98]

Campaigning on the Burma issue is ongoing. The Burma Campaign UK is currently targeting Premier Oil for its exploration work and investments in Burma. It is also urging consumer boycotts of Triumph International, under the slogan 'support breasts - not dictators', for manufacturing bras in Burma, and even Lonely Planet travel guides for publishing a guide to Burma and thereby facilitating tourism to Burma.[99] The campaigns against tourism to Burma have been so successful that the international style hotels operating in Rangoon apparently have occupancy rates of only 15 to 20 per cent.[100]

Unocal, the Taliban and Afghanistan

One of the corporations investing in Burma, the US oil company Unocal, has also been subject to a class action in the US courts concerning alleged human rights abuses by the Burmese government in the areas in which it was operating.[101] Class actions have become a major tool in campaigns against specific corporations and are used far more broadly than just the well known cases of suits against tobacco companies. Unocal was also subject to a similarly motivated campaign, long before September 11th when the Taliban and al-Qaida became the lead items on the nightly news, over its involvement in Afghanistan. Between 1995 and 1998, Unocal was part of a consortium that was planning to build a gas pipeline across Afghanistan. The pipeline was to transport gas from Turkmenistan's gas fields, across Afghanistan, to where there was a market for it in Pakistan.

The Taliban took control of Kabul and most of Afghanistan in 1996. The Taliban's appalling treatment of women soon became a major issue for US feminist groups. Unocal's involvement in the pipeline came in for fierce criticism and was subject to a vociferous campaign by American women's rights organisations. Unocal's response was, that by its presence in Afghanistan, it could improve the lot of women in Afghanistan. It, for example, promised to employ women on the project, made an issue of the treatment of women in its dealings with the Taliban, and funded community projects in Afghanistan. The other foreign companies involved at the time in pipeline projects in Afghanistan were Argentine and, perhaps more pertinently, Saudi Arabian, and made less of these human rights issues.

The more general point is that it is precisely large Western firms, ie, those most easily targeted and amenable to pressure from campaigns, which are most likely to be accountable for their actions, have precise and rigorous codes of conduct and insist on better employment and also environmental practices. When these Western firms pull out, they are often replaced by other companies which are less concerned with these issues and are also more difficult to hold to account. This argument, however, does not have the obvious moral attractiveness of calls for not investing in countries where serious human rights abuses are occurring.

The campaign against Unocal even asked the Californian Attorney General to have Unocal dissolved for this reason amongst others. Initiating moves to dissolve a company, or have a corporate charter revoked, has become a favourite tool in targeting corporations; it is largely a publicity-seeking or issue-raising exercise, since it has little practical chance of success. Unocal became the symbolic totem of concern for the women of Afghanistan. Its involvement in Afghanistan was interestingly as much of an issue as the US government's own ambivalent relationship with the Taliban regime in its early years.

The Clinton Government's relations with the Taliban worsened, according to leading commentator on Afghan affairs Ahmed Rashid, largely because of pressure from women's rights organisations, especially Feminist Majority. Osama Bin Laden's presence in Afghanistan was at this stage apparently a secondary issue. In the light of these worsening relations and the continuing onslaught upon the company by Feminist Majority and others, and the bad publicity these campaigns engendered, Unocal withdrew from the pipeline consortium in 1998.[102]

The campaign against Unocal shows how companies have today become the target of campaigns which would previously largely have been aimed at governments. For all the rhetoric of companies becoming ever more powerful, campaigners seem to realise that corporations are often more amenable to pressure than governments. This is even true when the issue is as far removed from, and has as little to do with, the boardrooms of America as the burqas Afghan women were forced to wear by the Taliban.

Ilisu Dam and Balfour Beatty

In the UK, an example of how effective the targeting of corporations for such ends can be even when there is no obvious consumer brand to boycott is the case of the construction firm Balfour Beatty and the Ilisu dam in Turkey. Here again a company - Balfour Beatty - was attacked as a proxy for a government. The Turkish Government wished to construct a dam on the Tigris River in an area of the country predominantly populated by the minority Kurdish population, who have long campaigned for independence or at least autonomy. The Ilisu dam was attacked for its alleged environmental impact, and because it would have displaced, depending on which figures one chooses to believe, up to 30,000 or 78,000 people. It would also have drowned various sites of historical importance to the Kurdish people.

An international consortium of construction firms, including Balfour Beatty, was to have built the dam. Balfour Beatty asked the British Government, through the mechanism of Export Credit Guarantees, to underwrite its £200 million contract for this project. The UK government said it was minded to do this in 1999, subject to various human rights and environmental criteria being satisfied. Balfour Beatty faced a massive campaign against its involvement in this project, spearheaded by Friends of the Earth and the London based Kurdish Human Rights Project.

The campaign also became something of a rallying cry for anti-capitalists. It is an example of how an issue can gain support from those trying to stop a specific project and raise concerns about a specific subject, dam building, and also from those trying to use it as an example of the evils of capitalism. Why state-sponsored dam building should be seen as a specifically capitalist vice, especially since its most vociferous adherents were a group hardly known for their capitalist ardour - planners in the Soviet Union and their overseas economic advisers and acolytes - is never properly explained.

In 2001 Balfour Beatty pulled out of the Ilisu dam project, saying it had failed to meet the company's ethical, environmental and commercial criteria.[103] Although not the sole factor and played down by the company itself, arguably the most important reason for Balfour Beatty's decision was the vociferous campaign against the company. Certainly the activist community saw this decision as a victory for their campaign. Mark Thomas, anti-capitalist television comedian and campaigner, put it thus: 'The proposed Ilisu dam is dead! We've won!'.[104] The anti-dam campaigners notched up further victories with the withdrawal of the dam's Italian contractors, Impregilo, and, in February 2002, UBS, Switzerland's largest bank group, withdrew their financial support from the dam. UBS cited concerns about the dam's social and environmental impact for their decision.[105]

The Ilisu dam project affected a very substantial contract for Balfour Beatty, and is in the core area of the company's activities. This is not an example of a company pulling out of a peripheral business activity. The campaigners were not calling for more account to be taken of environmental or human rights consider-ations but for the company to entirely pull out of the project. These factors, combined with the extra difficulty of targeting Balfour Beatty compared to a more visible consumer brand, would make one think that this is the least likely campaign against a company to succeed. The fact that it was a success shows just how powerful a campaigning tool the targeting of specific corporations has become. If it is true that a company such as Balfour Beatty can be successfully targeted, it is all the more true of high street consumer brands. The fear companies have of damaging their reputations has meant that campaigning organisations have become massively more powerful at the expense of corporations in general, and especially at the expense of consumer brands.

Campaigners who see the market as 'the only game in town'
The second category of campaigns not primarily motivated by the ideology of anti-branding are the significant numbers of organisations and activists who may have much sympathy with the wider anti-branding arguments, but believe that they are not realistic. They feel that since the consumer society is, so to speak, the only game in town, more can be achieved by playing along with it and cajoling or persuading corporations to change their practices. This group of organisations include many of the well established, household name NGOs and itself consists of a diverse spectrum. Some, such as Greenpeace International and Friends of the Earth are more confrontational - indeed, when they feel the circumstances demand it, very confrontational - but are willing to sit down with corporations when they feel it is appropriate. Greenpeace International and Friends of the Earth are, for example, currently behind The Body Shop endorsed Stop Esso Campaign calling for a boycott of ExxonMobil and its consumer brand Esso. The rationale behind this campaign is firstly that ExxonMobil have funded research and organisations, such as the Global Climate Coalition and the American Petroleum Institute, which are sceptical about man's contribution to global warming.

Secondly it is that, unlike the huge investments of other oil companies such as BP and Greenpeace International's erstwhile foe Shell,[106] ExxonMobil are not investing sufficiently in renewable energy and research into energy alternatives.[107] The leading *Guardian* columnist and voice of liberal Britain, Polly Toynbee, endorses the campaign not so much for what it will do to ExxonMobil, but as a consciousness-raising exercise to draw attention to what she believes is Britain's over-reliance on oil, and historic under-investment in renewables.[108]

Such consciousness-raising efforts, and attempts to move the public debate in a specific direction are often as much the motive in boycott campaigns of this type as any direct impact upon the company. They also have the advantage for the campaigners that they often persuade other corporations which have not been targeted to change their behaviour for fear of being next in line.

For this type of organisation, alongside the stick of boycott campaigns, there is also the carrot of co-operation. Greenpeace International is happy to say nice things about some corporations. It is, for example, much friendlier towards Shell than it once was, and has endorsed IKEA's stand on the sourcing of its wood products to ensure that they do not come from ancient forests, and also IKEA's decision to withdraw all PVC products from its stores.[109] The rhetoric of Greenpeace International and Friends of the Earth is increasingly that they are not against capitalism and the market *per se*, but that they want to move toward a more eco-aware market where corporations grasp the vast commercial opportunities offered by new environmentally friendly technologies and the demands of 'ethically aware' consumers.

Other organisations, such as Jonathan Porritt's Forum for the Future, are consistently more intent on quiet dialogue and are attacked for this by many more radical campaigners, such as George Monbiot.[110] Des Wilson, formerly head of Friends of the Earth and then corporate affairs director of the British airports operator, BAA, argues that greens 'have a better chance of promoting change by working with business and industry, instead of engaging in the kind of invariably useless confrontational activity enjoyed by the punk end of the movement.'[111]

It would be wrong, however, to see a clear divide between those who seek to reform the consumer society and those who wish to replace it. For, however much the anti-branders like the notion of a dichotomised world, these two strands of activism blend seamlessly into one another. Just as anti-branding organisations may receive support from some corporations and many individual anti-branders arc still ambiguously attached to 'fair trade', 'ethical' consumerism and its associated brands, more moderate campaigners share much, although not all, of the anti-branders' world view. Even Jonathan Porritt, who has also been head of Friends of the Earth, and was at one point the leading voice of radical environmentalism in the UK but is now widely seen as the unofficial environmental adviser to Prince Charles, acknowledges that his analysis still has much in common with that of the radicals. He says 'thank God for that absolutism! Over the last 10 years, I have learned just how much those working "the inside track" - with companies or government - depend on those hammering from the outside. Many of the companies we work with, for instance, live in dread of being targeted . . . and that's no bad thing.'[112]

If a general ideological distinction can be ascertained between the anti-branders and these other campaigners, it is that the latter are more likely to see materialism *per se* as the problem. They also tend not see this materialism as being purely the result of the machinations of the brands, and feel that consumers as a whole share responsibility for it. Thus for them the corporations alone are not the villains; wider social attitudes also need to change.

Campaigners who wish to close down a specific industry

The final category consists of those campaigners who are targeting individual corporations with the intention of closing down a specific industry, which they believe to be inherently immoral. Some of these campaigners may share the anti-branders' anti-capitalist outlook, but their objectives are not the same.

A classic example of a campaign which is seeking to shut down specific industries is that of the radical animal rights organisations, such as the US based PETA - People for the Ethical Treatment of Animals. This is a campaigning organisation, with a budget of almost $18 million in 2000,[113] which seeks an end to the fur trade, the livestock industry, zoos, and much else that they perceive as the exploitation of, or as cruelty to, animals. PETA has, for example, persuaded Marks & Spencer, amongst many other retailers, to stop selling products made from Indian leather, because of how cattle are allegedly treated in India.[114] In the UK, PETA are probably best known for persuading various super models to pose in the nude as part of an anti-fur campaign and their 'Crap on Ken' campaign against Mayor of London Ken Livingstone for withdrawing the licence of Trafalgar Square's pigeon feed vendor, the birds' primary source of food.

PETA has also targeted Coca-Cola for planning to market milk to children. PETA describes milk as a 'cruel, racist drink' (they claim that 'milk is a health hazard' and that 'most African-Americans and racial minorities are lactose-intolerant'), and argue that 'promoting it to children is tantamount to child abuse'. They call upon Coca-Cola to promote soy-based products instead.[115] Their objection is to milk itself, not primarily because of any health risks they might perceive, but because it is an integral part of the livestock industry. Unlike the anti-branders it is not to Coca-Cola, its marketing, or the use of lifestyle images to sell drinks that they object. PETA are more than happy for soy milk, or any other vegan product, to be aggressively promoted in such a manner.

A campaign which is in the same class, albeit closer to mainstream prejudices while simultaneously being somewhat more esoteric, is Greenpeace International's successful strategy of quietly persuading 21 major airlines flying out of Norway to refuse to transport blubber or whale meat.[116] This is part of their ongoing campaign against whaling. Such campaigns are not directed at discrediting consumerism itself, but at putting an end to practices, and in some cases whole sectors of the economy, of which the campaigners disapprove.

Greenpeace International's whaling strategy is just one example of campaigners approaching third parties - companies that are not directly involved - in order to get at their real target. This strategy is usually employed by those who seek to target a specific industry which itself, such as the Norwegian whaling industry, is not amenable to pressure. A UK or US boycott of whaling produce is unlikely to have very much impact.

The campaign against Huntingdon Life Sciences
An altogether more sinister example of this kind of strategy has been employed by the militant British animal rights group, SHAC or Stop Huntingdon Animal Cruelty.[117] The Huntingdon Life Sciences corporation carries out experiments for medical research on a contractual basis; half this research is carried out on animals. SHAC realised it would not get very far by trying to persuade or put pressure upon a company one of whose primary business activities is animal experimentation to quit animal experimentation. So it decided to target the pension funds and other collective investments which held shares in Huntingdon Life Sciences, the banks which operated nominee accounts through which individuals or pension funds could hold shares in Huntingdon Life Sciences, the banks which lent money to the company, and even individual private shareholders.[118]

This was a remarkably successful operation. One by one, vast UK and US corporations caved in and refused to have anything to do with Huntingdon Life Sciences, many to the extent of not even handling shares in the company for their clients: Barclays Bank, Citigroup, HSBC, Merill Lynch, Charles Schwab, TD Waterhouse. The Royal Bank of Scotland refused further funding to the company. Huntingdon Life Sciences was only saved from closure due to moral support from the UK Labour Government's Science Minister, Lord Sainsbury, and funding from a US investment firm with a low public profile in the UK, the Arkansas-based Stephens Group. Since then, various pharmaceutical companies and medical research charities have threatened to withdraw their accounts from the banks which gave into the animal rights activists' demands.[119]

SHAC's campaign has come very close to achieving its aim of destroying Huntingdon Life Sciences, and it is continuing. SHAC's supporters in the USA have targeted the Stephens Group. This company has now also withdrawn its support for Huntingdon Life Sciences, although it says this decision was a purely commercial one.[120] If SHAC ever succeeds in closing Huntingdon Life Sciences down they will move on and seek to destroy others who are involved in the work of animal experimentation.

SHAC employed all manner of strategies in their campaign. These included using the techniques of anti-branding in their leaflets and on their web sites in associating the retail banks with the negative image of animal experimentation and its alleged cruelty, and thereby selling their extremist message to a wider, senti-mentalist, audience. SHAC's objectives, however, were far more specific and thus amenable to a clearer outcome. The actions of these animal rights extremists is illustrative of how a small, well-organised campaign can intimidate some of the largest corporations in the world, the very corporations which the anti-corporate activists claim are engaged in a global corporate power grab. Polly Toynbee described the behaviour of the banks and finance houses in not standing up to SHAC thus: 'The cowardice is breathtaking. At the first whiff of gunpowder the captains of industry, the big banks, stockbrokers, financiers . . . turned tail and fled'.[121]

Established campaigners have better access to the media than corporations
In all these three categories, the established, seemingly moderate, campaigners have, contrary to widespread perception, the advan-tage that their voice is far more clearly heard in the media than that of the corporations. A study by the highly respected Brookings Institution of press coverage in the liberal *New York Times*, conservative *Wall Street Journal* and the more specialist *Congressional Quarterly Weekly Report* shows that 'corporate

representatives are a mere one per cent of all lobbyists quoted by the reporters for these three outlets'.[122] While it is true that corporations' voices are heard more clearly via trade associations, who receive 30.1 per cent of such coverage, 46.2 per cent of lobbyists quoted are from citizens' group, overwhelmingly liberal, progressive citizens groups. What is more, representatives of such liberal, progressive organisations are far less likely to be described in pejorative terms than others, especially corporate representatives.[123]

The targeting of corporations by non-progressive campaigns
While most of the examples of campaigns so far given are generally perceived, rightly or otherwise, as progressive causes, the politics of those targeting an individual corporation are not necessarily progressive. Pro-death penalty, anti-crime campaigners, for example, successfully targeted Sears, the second largest US retailer. Sears had launched a private label line in its department stores for fashion brand Benetton, which was expected to generate $100 million in sales in its first year. Benetton is known for its topical hard-hitting advertising and decided to run an advertising campaign critical of the death penalty featuring death row prisoners. The campaigners succeeded in getting Sears to sever its contract with Benetton.[124] Benetton has also had to apologise to families of US murder victims and has paid $50,000 compensation to a fund for victims of crime in Missouri.[125]

The USA's largest retailer Wal-Mart is subject to a boycott campaign by those who still have an emotional sympathy with the long lost Confederate cause. Wal-Mart will no longer stock Piggie Park barbecue sauces because Piggie Park's owner, Maurice Bessinger, likes to fly the Confederate flag of the southern rebel states outside his restaurants.[126]

Having said all this, anti-branding is perhaps the most important reason why individual corporations are being targeted, and why the targeting of corporations is becoming ever more prevalent. It has turned attacks upon corporations from merely a mechanism for achieving some other demand into the major ideological tool of those seeking to proselytise for their anti-capitalist faith. But does it succeed in doing this?

5
The Fallacies of Anti-Branding

Anti-branding as an activists' tool - the medium becomes the message

Anti-branding is a marketing device, and suffers from all the weaknesses inherent in such devices. The attack on individual corporations is only the medium, but the medium ends up becoming the message. For what does anti-branding achieve? It succeeds in damaging the reputation of this or that brand. It might even damage the sales of this or that brand. However, no more than a tiny fraction of those who, for example, register the attacks upon Nike will end up adopting a thorough-going anti-capitalist ideology. This is perhaps not surprising since the anti-branders themselves adopt such a mish-mash of ideologies. But even the idea that the anti-branders are all agreed upon, a rejection of consumerism, is unlikely to be instilled in more than a few.

The most widespread response of those registering these campaigns will be to still buy a pair of Nike trainers, just to feel a tinge of guilt about it, or to decide, well, let's buy another brand of trainers. As Klein acknowledges, Reebok has 'rushed to capitalise on Nike's controversies by positioning itself as the ethical shoe alternative . . . to make sure that consumers find what they are looking for in Reebok, the company has taken to handing out high-profile Reebok Human Rights Awards to activists who fight against child labour and repressive regimes.'[127] To further underline their commitment to human rights, Reebok have, along with musician Peter Gabriel and the Lawyers Committee for Human Rights, founded an organisation called Witness. This provides hand-held video cameras to 'front-line' activists so that they can document human rights abuses.[128]

The Reebok/Nike case is not an isolated incident. The discomfort of one company is often a boon to its competitors. The anti-branders are thus, while trying to discredit all major corporations, succeeding in boosting the sales of some corporations at the expense of others. This is all very well for the kind of activists whose aim it is to make a given company change a specific policy or practice, but clearly achieves very little for those who are trying to bring about a rejection of the ethos of consumption.

Anti-branding has become popular because it has learnt to utilise popular prejudices

Anti-branding has popular resonance because, just like the brands, it has learnt to utilise popular prejudices. One need only look at the anti-branders' favoured targets. McDonald's, for example, while its customers continue to pour in, has long been at the receiving end of all kinds of urban myths. Many when surveyed seem to believe urban myths about McDonald's - such as McDonald's apocryphal 'funding of the IRA' and their supposed 'cutting down of the tropical rain forests and killing endangered species' - and, what is more, 'know' them to be 'true'. These claims are, quite simply, nonsense. However, showing up these ludicrous allegations for the fabrications that they are will not shift the widespread belief in the truth of them and other, similar, claims. They, after all, make for a much better story than mundane reality does.

McDonald's has been a pet hate of myriad people ranging from folk-weavers who will only eat 'natural food', whatever that may be, to suburban housewives who feel that McDonald's is vulgar and the opening of a new branch down the road will lower the tone of the neighbourhood. When the McLibel Two pillory McDonald's or French farmer activist José Bové smashes up a branch of McDonald's while it is under construction,[129] they become heroic figures for many who do not remotely share their wider politics. It is hardly surprising that these figures find such a receptive audience. They are not challenging popular perceptions, but confirming them. This does not, however, mean that suburban housewives will be converted to anti-consumerism, let alone green anarchism.

McDonald's is an extreme example. More generally, however, attacks on the multi-national corporations behind the brands are likely to find receptive audiences. This is because large numbers of the public are willing to believe virtually any myth about large corporations. The public is simultaneously facing in two directions on this issue. While it is very keen on the brands these corporations provide and trusts the goods they buy from them, at the same time large corporations are widely perceived as distant, greedy and powerful - and thus somewhat sinister. Contrary to the anti-branders' claims, anti-branding is not challenging a general atmosphere where the brands have manipulated the public into believing that the big corporations behind the brands are on 'their' side. It is simply reinforcing popular anti-corporate, anti-big business prejudices. Nor, to any significant extent, is anti-branding achieving its aim in spreading a broader anti-capitalist ideology. The irony is that, whilst large corporations as a species are widely disliked and the public is willing to believe all kinds of claims about them, the success of the brands themselves is based upon trust and its corollary, reputation.

The true basis of branding - an instant source of information
The anti-branders misinterpret the function of branding. Only in certain instances is it a means of projecting a youthful, rebellious or caring image upon a particular corporation's products. Even in those instances, that is not all branding is. Much more importantly branding is an extremely useful invention in that it transmits a vast amount of information to the consumer in an instant. Without branding the consumer would have to go into each and every purchase blind. For branding is a body of accumulated knowledge. This knowledge may often have been obtained through advertising, but then the product must correspond, and live up to, the consumer's expectations. Even Klein acknowledges, that if a product does not live up to consumers' expectations, in this case the 1998 film Godzilla, however good its advertising, its wider marketing and its supposedly foolproof synergistic strategies, it will not succeed. 'None of this could compensate for the simple fact that nearly everyone who saw Godzilla warned their friends to stay away, and they did, in droves.'[130] Consumer brands rely on repeat purchases from their customers for their continued success. It is thus even more important for consumer brands than for films to live up to their customers' expectations. Branding means that consumers know what they can expect to obtain when making a purchase. It is a form of quality assurance for the customer. It is regulation by the market place.

The anti-branders, through concentrating their attacks on the kinds of youth-oriented brands which appeal to the activists' own target audience, ignore the breadth and scope of branding. They ignore the importance of brands in nearly every other facet of the economy. From house repairs to antique dealing, newspapers to universities, corporate finance to insurance, branding is central. Some of these brands, such as highly specialist retailers, may be minute and amount to one shop. Others are vast. They all, however, perform the same function. They give the consumer instant information.

Companies in every sector of the economy seek to build up a reputation for their products and use this reputation, whatever it might be in the specific instance, to boost their sales. If they do not live up to this reputation, they might for a while be able to live on their past reputation, but they will indubitably eventually be punished by the market place. Branding thus encourages corporations to provide a good product and deliver what their customer desire.

The rise of certification as another form of branding

It is interesting how, when companies are unable to build up a strong enough reputation on their own, groups of companies often band together or seek the endorsement of a third party to obtain some of the reputational advantages of branding. This phenomenon can be seen in the specialist craft associations that exist for everything from butchers to picture framers. Just as with branding, customers know what they can expect, in this case a certain quality of service and product, by using the members of such associations.

The phenomenon can also be seen in the endless certification schemes running today assuring customers that such and such a product meets such and such a standard, the standard frequently being of an environmental or ethical nature. These schemes cover a diverse range of issues. To list but a few of these certification schemes: FairTrade certifies that Southern producers are being paid reasonably for their produce; the Forest Stewardship Council that the wood used in a product is being harvested sustainably; and the Soil Association that produce is organic.[131] There is even a proposed scheme in the UK to certify the safety of sex aids.[132] All such schemes are an attempt to gain the advantages of branding.

The fact is that progressive middle-class opinion finds it more palatable to want to obtain instant information about how a vegetable has been grown than to know what a burger and fries will taste like, and how long it will take to be served, before entering a food outlet. This does not, however, make the former any less an example of branding than the latter. The desire for either piece of instant information is no less 'valid' than for the other. Both are forms of quality assurance and market regulation. This role of branding is tacitly acknowledged by much radical opinion in their support for the legalisation of currently illegal drugs.

The legalisation of drugs: the tacit acknowledgement of the benefits of branding by radical opinion

Calls for the legalisation of some or all drugs have considerably moved toward the political mainstream. In Britain, the former Conservative Cabinet Minister Peter Lilley has called for the legalisation of cannabis,[133] *The Economist* has called for all drugs to be legalised,[134] and the influential House of Commons Home Affairs Select Committee of backbench MPs has called for the drug laws to be liberalised.[135] However campaigners for the legalisation of drugs, especially ecstasy and cannabis, in general still tend to be people who see themselves as radicals. Indeed they often see the prohibition of drugs as somehow an establishment conspiracy, and strongly identify themselves with the ethos of anti-branding campaigns and the notion of ever increasing corporate power.

One of the main arguments for a change in the law is that if drugs were legalised those that choose to consume currently illegal drugs would know what they were obtaining, and know that it was of a certain quality, ie, the drugs would not be adulterated with noxious substances. Is not the progressive opinion that espouses such views acknowledging the benefits of branding? Are they not in fact calling for the branding of drugs? The quasi-branding of ecstasy is already occurring in the proliferation of different varieties of ecstasy, such as White Doves, Rhubarb and Custards, or, in an echo of legitimate brands appropriating radical chic, Malcolm Xs.[136]

This emergence of quasi-brands may point to how powerful and useful a tool branding is in that it even emerges in the least auspicious of circumstances. Such quasi-brands in illegal goods, however, obviously have none of the advantages of real brands: the brands have no legal protection and there is thus not only the certainty of unhindered, unrestrictable counterfeiting but there is also no incentive to maintain quality as anyone can manufacture the product. The benefits that are ascribed to the legalisation of drugs are obviously partly simply the consequence of moving from an illegal to a legal market. There are, however, also, and perhaps more importantly, the benefits which would accrue from the emergence of real, legal brands in such currently illegal substances. Next time radicals think of marching for the legalisation of cannabis or ecstasy, they should consider that they are in fact extolling the benefits of branding and corporatisation.

Ironically, if this were to happen these protesters would probably soon be highlighting the long term health risks associated with cannabis and the very real dangers of ecstasy. This is borne out by the way many people who see tobacco companies as the incarnation of evil for pushing a noxious substance somehow see those pushing another noxious substance, cannabis, as harbingers of freedom. This is even though tobacco companies operate in a legal framework which tightly constrains their actions and holds them to account, while peddlers of illegal substances have no such accountability. Progressive opinion seems to prefer to put its trust in gangsters rather than multinational corporations.

Anti-branding represents the dumbing down of anti-capitalism

What then of the claims that brands are pernicious because they sell a particular lifestyle? As argued previously, branding is about much more than simply selling an association with a lifestyle. On occasions, however, association with a particular lifestyle is undoubtedly part of what the consumer is trying to obtain. Consumers may wish to be identified as a certain type of person and may consume products accordingly. Although this is undoubtedly exploited by brands, it is not a phenomenon of branding. All kinds of decisions about taste are connected with how individuals perceive themselves and wish others to perceive them. It is undeniable that whether someone cultivates an interest in opera and Austen, or in dog racing and soap operas, or for that matter in anti-capitalist protest is partly a question of how that person wishes to be perceived by others and the type of lifestyle that person wishes to be associated with. The relationship between what one consumes and questions of lifestyle is not intrinsically one of branding. It is a far more deep seated phenomenon.

Earlier anti-capitalists were aware of this. They too, of course, had to find a reason for hating capitalism. They thus argued that the bourgeoisie constructed what was good taste and what was not, what was high art and what was low, what was refined and what was vulgar, as a means of maintaining their own power. Through their control and construction of culture, the argument went, the bourgeoisie maintained their iron control on society. This was the essential argument of authors from Thorstein Veblen, writing at the end of the nineteenth century, in his *The Theory of the Leisure Class*[137] to Pierre Bourdieu, who died in 2002 and was seen by some as the last of the French public intellectuals of the left in the tradition of Jean Paul Sartre,[138] in his *Distinction - A Social Critique of the Judgement of Taste*[139]. The argument, with this or that variation, is in fact still often heard today in Marxist and Marxisant academic discourse.

The anti-branders have, however, replaced this sophisticated and subtle, if erroneous, argument with a simplistic, naive and equally false one. Instead of arguing that questions of judgement and taste are complex phenomena which are somehow controlled by a ruling class in their own interests, such questions have been reduced to attacks upon Nike's advertising budget. This is not the only instance of how today's protesters seem afraid of complex arguments. As this examination of the anti-corporate movement shows, anti-branding is a marketing device for a wider anti-capitalist message. The necessity to put forward a clear simple message to sell a product, in this case anti-capitalism, has meant that that product has itself been simplified. What this amounts to is the dumbing down of anti-capitalism.

Brands are not impregnable

Perhaps as a corollary of concentrating in their attacks, albeit as a marketing device, upon the alleged iniquities of individual corporations rather than putting forward a wholesale critique of capitalism as a system from the start, the notion has arisen that individual corporations and their brands have become impregnable. This is another case of how the medium of anti-branding has become the message itself. The notion of the impregnable brand is, however, itself false.

Today's powerful brands often had humble origins

What is interesting is that those brands which are most widely attacked are not those set up by some large multi-national after extensive market research and heavy reliance upon focus groups. They are those which, from small beginnings, have risen to become what they are today through offering a new innovative product which has caught the public imagination. McDonald's is perhaps the prime example of this. As the highly critical history *Fast Food Nation*[140] records, McDonald's started with a single drive-in restaurant in 1937. In 1948, its founders, the McDonald brothers, came up with the revolutionary idea of eliminating most items from their menu, scrapping knives, forks, and plates, and introducing a conveyor belt style kitchen. This was the first place to take the principles of factory line production and apply them to food. It meant that going out to buy food became affordable to all Americans. It also sought to attract families, rather than just the usual clientele of adolescents that were the mainstay of US diners at the time. A small time salesman of milkshake mixers, Ray Kroc, then came up with the idea of franchising McDonald's and its innovative 'Speedee Service System' across America.

Eric Schlosser, *Fast Food Nation*'s author, goes on to record how Dunkin' Donuts, Wendy's, Kentucky Fried Chicken, Burger King (then called Insta-Burger King), and Domino's Pizza all had similar humble beginnings in the years after World War II. Kentucky Fried Chicken, for example, acquired its Colonel Saunders mascot because its founder could not afford to advertise his new food outlet, so as a publicity stunt, dressed up as a Kentucky Colonel.[141] Obviously many other attempts to establish fast food chains failed to catch the public imagination. Those that succeeded did so because they offered the public a product they wanted at an affordable price, were at the right place at the right time, and were truly innovative. Many of these innovations, whatever one may think of the finished fast food product, are indubitably works of genius. This is why they succeeded. They did not have the backing of vast corporations, and did not break through due to their commercial size and power, advantages that they quite simply did not have in their early days.

Other consumer brands have obviously been launched by vast corporations using the whole panoply of modern methods of market research. However, companies with innovative ideas that catch the public imagination can today still grow from small beginnings into prevalent high street brands. The Body Shop, having secured a £4,000 bank loan, started with one shop in Brighton in 1976.[142] Many other leading brands, including Nike, Ben & Jerry's, Reebok, Esprit, Pizza Express, The Gap, had similarly humble origins. If brands such as McDonald's and The Body Shop can rise from nothing to what they are today, so can others.

Leading brands can also be challenged and decline as rapidly as they rose. Marks & Spencer, once one of the mainstays of British shopping, famously hit difficulties. This decline was often blamed in media reports on the merciless onslaught by the brands. Such reporting supposes that Marks & Spencer is somehow not a brand itself. One of the brands which was seen as spearheading the onslaught on the traditional High Street, The Gap, was itself reported to have lost some of its lustre, and showed a marked down-turn in profits, in autumn 2001.[143]

Various league-tables of the world's top brands, in terms of monetary value, are drawn up every year. What is interesting is the frequency with which the corporations that appear in these league-tables change. Moreover, the rate at which they change is increasing. *The Economist* records, looking at league tables of the top 100 corporate brands in 2000 and 2001, that 74 brands appear in both lists. Of these, 41 fell in monetary value in the year, and the combined value of the 74 brands fell by $49 billion, a drop of more than five per cent.[144] This is hardly evidence for the popular image of the ever-growing power, and remorseless onward march, of the brands.

Large companies are not increasing their share of overall economic activity

Furthermore, looking at large companies in general, far from becoming ever larger and thus pushing out smaller businesses, in the USA there is clear evidence that they have declined in relative terms as a percentage of the whole economy. From the 1980s to the mid-1990s, *The Statistical Abstract of the United States* recorded data on the top 500 corporations in the USA, the so-called Fortune 500. Comparing this data with figures for the US economy as a whole, it shows that the Fortune 500 share of total US assets fell from 15.4 per cent in 1980 to 12.3 per cent in 1993. This represents a decline of over 20 per cent.

While in absolute terms, even indexed for inflation, the value of assets these corporations held increased dramatically over this period, it fell as a percentage because the value of assets held by other firms increased even more rapidly. Looking at the numbers of those employed by these firms as a percentage of total US employment, this declined even more rapidly from 16 per cent in

1980 to 11.3 per cent in 1993. Even these declines do not paint the whole picture, since the companies that constitute the top 500 companies have changed substantially over the period.[145] This again paints a rather different picture than the popularly conceived perception of the largest corporations gobbling up ever more of the country. It undermines the activists' talk of a creeping corporate take-over of the whole of society by the largest corporations.

A favourite tool employed by anti-corporate activists to dramatise their fears of ever growing corporate power is to compare the size of various companies with the size of the economies of various countries. These comparisons frequently rely on data from the Institute for Policy Studies in Washington, DC. In a widely cited report, The Institute for Policy Studies seeks to show that, of the world's 100 largest economies, 51 are corporations and of the world's 50 largest economies, 14 are corporations.[146]

The eminent economic commentator, Martin Wolf of the *Financial Times*, has pointed out, by drawing on the work of two Belgian economists, that these comparisons do not compare like with like. The size of companies is measured by total sales, and the size of economies by GDP. These are measures of two quite different things. GDP is a measure of value added; if one were to measure the size of a country's economy by total sales one would have a very much larger figure. By measuring the size of companies by value added, ie, the same way the economies of countries are measured, a proper comparison of the size of companies and the size of the economies of countries can be made. By this measure the number of companies among the top 100 economies is reduced to 37, and among the top 50 economies, only two are companies. Anti-corporate activists like to repeat the Institute for Policy Studies' claim that GM, perhaps still better known as General Motors - for many years America's largest company and in 2001 America's, and the world's, third largest company in terms of revenue[147] - is bigger than Denmark's economy. Properly measured the economy of Denmark is three times the size of GM, and GM is in fact smaller than the economy of Bangladesh.[148] This does not somehow have quite the same resonance.

Small companies are not necessarily driven out by large brands

Related to the notion of the invincible brand, is the idea that brands force smaller companies out of the market. Undoubtedly there has been much consolidation in many markets. However in areas where large corporations are especially strong, niche markets can still develop and there is room for far smaller competitors. In a market that is dominated by large corporations small-scale operations can still prosper, if they serve a particular demand for which the major players do not, or are incapable of, catering.

We are not witnessing a relentless march toward homogenisation without any countervailing influences. For example, in the UK the real ale movement led to a revival in small-scale brewers. This was a reaction to the increased homogenisation of beer. In the UK over 300 new breweries producing real ale are now operating.[149] Many of these may be very small scale, but that is the whole point. It shows that small operations can survive, even grow and flourish, in markets with powerful brands. A similar thing has also happened in the UK and USA with the rise of farmhouse cheeses.

A more recent trend in the UK is the rise of Farmers' Markets. In a reaction against the perceived power of supermarkets and large-scale agri-business, Farmers' Markets have been set up in many towns where local farmers can sell their produce directly to consumers. Only goods produced locally may be sold at Farmers' Markets. In 1997 the first UK Farmers' Market was established. In 2001 there were nearly 200.[150] Just like McDonald's, the Farmers' Market movement is a US import to the UK. In the USA, where the movement had its origins in the 1970s, there are over 3,000 Farmers' Markets, selling over $1 billion in fresh produce every year.[151] Farmers' Market will clearly not replace the large supermarkets, real ale will not replace Budweiser, but, contrary to widespread perception, both can thrive simultaneously.

6

Brands and The South

Globalisation is improving the lives of the poor in the South
The issue perhaps most often raised by the anti-branders in their attacks upon the corporations is that corporate activity and globalisation is making the condition of the poor in the South worse. *The United Nations Human Development Report 2001*[152] tells a rather different story. It shows that much of the world still lives in horrific poverty: in the developing world 1.2 billion people live on less than $1 a day in purchasing power parity terms to a 1993 US dollar; 2.8 billion live on less than $2 a day; 325 million children do not go to school; more than 850 million are illiterate; 11 million children under five die each year from preventable causes; nearly a billion people do not have access to improved water sources; and 2.4 billion lack access to basic sanitation.[153]

The situation, contrary to the anti-branders claims, is, however, improving. Between 1975 and 1998 average incomes in developing countries almost doubled in real purchasing power parity terms from $1,300 to $2,500. Adult literacy has increased from 47 per cent in 1970 to 73 per cent in 1999. The number of rural families with access to clean water has grown more than fivefold, with 80 per cent of people in the developing world having access to improved water supplies. The number of undernourished people fell by 40 million between 1990-92 and 1996-98. Infant mortality has been reduced by more than 10 per cent from 1990 to 1999. The number of those living on less than $1 per day in constant terms, in spite of a rising world population, fell by 120 million between 1993 and 1998, and 200 million since 1980.[154] This represents the first fall in absolute numbers of those living in extreme poverty, ever. It does not reflect the anti-globalisers' claims of an ever worsening situation for the poor of the South. These reductions in poverty may seem trivial to some in comparison with the overall scale of the problem, but they are far from trivial to those involved. They can quite literally be a matter of life and death.

These improvements have not, however, occurred uniformly. To give just one indicator, in East Asia average incomes were one tenth of those in the OECD countries in 1960. By 1998, even though incomes in the OECD countries have increased massively, East Asian average incomes had reached nearly one fifth of those in the OECD countries. On the other hand, in Sub-Saharan Africa incomes in 1960 were slightly higher than in East Asia at one ninth of those in the OECD countries, in 1998 they were an eighteenth.[155] Research by the World Bank shows that the most significant factor in explaining such differentials is the degree to which countries have been integrated into the global economy. East Asian countries, by and large, have successfully integrated into the world economy; Sub-Saharan African countries, by and large, have not.

Those economies that have globalised most have seen the fastest rates of poverty alleviation - non-globalising economies have seen static, or rising rates of poverty

The World Bank's report, *Globalization, Growth and Poverty*[156], examines the economies of 24 globalising countries, which have integrated into the world economy since 1980, and 49 non-globalising countries, which are no more integrated into the global economy today than they were twenty years ago, and in many cases are less so. In the 1990s the globalisers had an average GDP per capita growth rate of 5 per cent, compared to 2.2 per cent in the rich countries, and 1.4 per cent in the non-globalisers. In 1980 the 24 countries embarking upon globalisation were poorer than the 49 non-globalisers.

Today the globalisers are richer. Anti-globalisation protesters will respond that GDP is not everything, and globalisation has reduced living standards, and increased poverty and inequalities. The World Bank study shows that 'in general, the more rapid growth that developing countries experience as they integrate with the global economy translates into poverty reduction . . . the only countries in which we have seen large-scale poverty reduction in the 1990s are ones that have become more open to foreign trade and investment'.[157] China has for example had the most dramatic poverty reduction in history since opening up its markets. In Vietnam, another leading globaliser, those living in absolute poverty have fallen from 75 per cent of the population in 1988 to 37 per cent in 1998.[158] Ninety eight per cent of the very poorest households in Vietnam became better off during the 1990s. They became better off because of the new opportunities offered in labour intensive industries, in the very sweatshop so strongly attacked by the anti-branders. This increased wealth has led to a fall in child labour and an increase in school enrolment.[159] In the globalising countries life expectancy, infant mortality and under-five mortality have all improved rapidly. These figures are fast approaching those prevalent in the West as recently as the 1960s.

Globalisation does not necessarily increase inequalities

Moving on to the issue of inequalities, the period of rapid globalisation since 1980 has been the first period of a reduction in global income inequality in over 200 years.[160] Within countries, the research shows that there is no systematic relationship between increased integration into the world economy and rising inequality. In some of the globalisers, such as Malaysia and the Phillipines, inequality of income has fallen. In others, such as Costa Rica and Vietnam, it has been stable. In yet others, especially China, inequalities have risen. The Chinese example, however, shows that rising inequalities are not necessarily a bad thing. China used to be very equal and very poor; now it is somewhat less equal and, as shown, somewhat less poor.[161] Whatever else may be said of China's Communist Party government and its appalling human rights record, its decision to open up and globalise the Chinese economy has undoubtedly benefited the Chinese people as a whole.

The presence of multinationals in the South tends to have a beneficial impact upon pay and working conditions

Within the South, those working for Western multinationals enjoy the highest incomes. In low income countries, wages in foreign affiliates to American owned companies are on average twice those of domestic manufacturing wages.[162] What of those not working for Western companies directly, but for companies supplying Western businesses and especially those supplying Western high street brands? The establishment of such factories supplying clothing and footwear to the West has been a first step on the route out of poverty for Hong Kong, Singapore, Korea and Taiwan.[163] A study for the respected Institute for International Economics shows that conditions in such factories vary tremendously. 'They varied greatly from plant to plant, from deplorable to commendable. In some, by any definition, sweatshop conditions did prevail. But in others it was

73

hard to find significant fault with working conditions. . . . The worst working conditions I observed were to be found in locally owned plants that did not serve the international market.'[164]

It is precisely the global brands, fearing for their reputations, which impose the most stringent conditions on their suppliers and insist on improved employment conditions. Making these companies pull out of the South would make the poor worse off. Kevin Watkins of the international development charity Oxfam puts it thus: 'There is no case you can point at where sanctions have improved labour standards. It's about a labour aristocracy in the North protecting its jobs and conditions.'[165] Do the campaigners really claim to know better what is in the interests of those working in the sweatshops than the workers themselves do? The sweatshops are an escape route from grinding rural poverty.

The new anti-capitalism has given new life to old, discredited claims

The anti-branding, anti-globalisation activists' romanticisation of conditions for the rural poor of the South working outside of the globalised economy shares much with Friedrich Engels' vision of the rural poor of England before the Industrial Revolution: 'They did not need to overwork; they did no more than they chose to do, and yet earned what they needed . . . work which, in itself, was recreation for them . . . games contributed to their physical health and vigour. They were "respectable" people, good husbands and fathers, led moral lives . . . The young people grew up in idyllic simplicity and intimacy with their playmates until they married.'[166]

This is not the only similarity the new protesters have with their predecessors. To answer the question raised at the start of the study, the new anti-capitalism does not offer any new, radical insights. Instead it reheats old, long discredited arguments. There are obviously some changes: corporations are still sometimes attacked for their conservatism, but more often for what the activists perceive as their feigned liberalism; the villains have, for most of today's protesters, ceased to be the bourgeoisie or capitalism *per se*, and have become the corporations instead; today's protesters, in general, do not believe they have all the answers, in fact they do not offer solutions; and very few of today's protesters believe that there was much in the 'real existing socialism' of the Soviet Union that is worth emulating.

Anti-branding should be understood as a marketing exercise, and as marketing exercises are prone to do, the message has both been made more amusing, more self-consciously clever and has been dumbed down. For many activists, the marketing, the anti-branding, has itself become the message; clever parodies and visual jokes are what it is about for them. The underlying motivations behind these campaigns - a belief that profit is immoral by definition, a blinkered vision of society as neatly dichotomised into the exploiting few and the exploited many, and a passionate commitment to equality of outcome regardless of consequence - however remain the same. It is an irony that, at a time when the achievements of capitalism are becoming ever more apparent, capitalism is on the defensive, while the manifest failures of anti-capitalism seem to have done little to diminish the ardour many have for finding 'an alternative'. Perhaps the wrong people are apologising.

Biographical note

Michael Mosbacher is Deputy Director of the Social Affairs Unit. He studied politics at Exeter University, writing his Master's dissertation on the impact of the collapse of communism in Eastern Europe and the Soviet Union upon the British Communist movement. He is Editor (with Digby Anderson) of *The British Woman Today: a qualitative survey of images in women's magazines* and *Another Country*. He is a contributor to *Scot-Free: How England would fare without Scotland* and *The Dictionary of Dangerous Words*.

Notes and references

1   Stephen Kotkin, *Armageddon Averted: The Soviet Collapse 1970-2000*, Oxford University Press, Oxford, 2001.

2   Paul Hollander, *Political Pilgrims - Western Intellectuals in Search of the Good Life*, Transaction Press, New Jersey, 1998.

3   Mike Mosbacher, *The British Communist Movement and Moscow: How The Demise of the Soviet Union Affected the Communist Party and its Successor Organisations*, www.libertarian.co.uk, London, 1996.

4   Francis Fukuyama, *The End of History and The Last Man*, Hamish Hamilton, London, 1992.

5   Francois Furet, *The Passing of an Illusion - The Idea of Communism in the Twentieth Century*, University of Chicago Press, Chicago/London, 1999, pp502-503.

6   Hollander, op cit.

7   Paul Foot, 'Putting the demo back in democracy', *London Review of Books*, February 14th 2001.

8   Donald Katz, *Just Do It - The Nike Spirit in the Corporate World*, Adams Media Corporation, Holbrook, Massachusetts, 1994, p7.

9   Naomi Klein, *No Logo*, Flamingo, an imprint of HarperCollins, London, 2000.

10 Bestsellers, *The Times*, 28th February 2001, Section 2, p9.

11 'What the world is reading', *The Economist*, 30th June 2001, p100.

12 Description of *No Logo*, amazon.co.uk.

13 'Pro-Logo: Brands, Who's wearing the trousers?', *The Economist*, 8th September 2001, cover and pp27-29.

14 Amazon.co.uk, op cit.

15 James Harkin, 'The Logos fight back', *New Statesman*, 18th June 2001.

16 Naomi Klein, 'Outflanking the rich and powerful', *The Guardian*, 26th January 2001, p22.

17 'Meanwhile, in another world - Bigger, yes. But any more influential?', *The Economist*, 7th February 2002.

18 Noreena Hertz, *The Silent Takeover - Global Capitalism and the Death of Democracy*, Heinemann, London, 2001.

19 George Monbiot, *Captive State - The Corporate Takeover of Britain*, Macmillan, London, 2000.

20 John Lloyd, *The Protest Ethic - How the anti-globalisation movement challenges social democracy*, Demos, London, 2001, p54.

21 Naomi Klein, 'Why Marcos is the Che Guevara of his generation - The Unknown Icon', *The Guardian*, March 3rd 2001, Weekend, pp9-14.

22 Hollander, op cit, Introduction to the Transaction Edition, pxvii.

23 Klein, op cit, 2000 p315.

24 Protest & Survive, *Whitechapel Art Gallery*, personal visit to exhibition and exhibition catalogue, Protest & Survive, Whitechapel Art Gallery, London, 2000.

25 Peter Marshall, *Demanding the Impossible - A History of Anarchism*, Fontana, an imprint of HarperCollins, London, 1993, p315.

26 Protest & Survive catalogue, ibid.

27 Benjamin M. Compaine & Douglas Gomery, *Who Owns the Media? Competition & Concentration in the Mass Media Industry*, Third Edition, Lawrence Erlbaum, New Jersey, 2000, p463-464.

28 Kerry A. Dolan and Luisa Kroll, 'Billionaires - The World's Richest People', *Forbes Global*, 9th July 2001.

29 Ed Vulliamy, 'The New Citizen Kane?', *The Observer*, 20th May 2001, p27.

30 Nicholas Wapshott, '$69m buys election as Mayor of New York', *The Times*, 5th December 2001, p9.

31 Digby Anderson, *Good Companies Don't Have Missions*, Social Affairs Unit, London, 2000.

32 Christopher Yablonski (ed), *Patterns of Corporate Philanthropy XII*, 1999, pp260-261.

33 Shelter website, 'Supporting Shelter - Corporate and Organisations', www.shelter.org.uk. See also John Smyth, *The Guide to UK Company Giving*, Third Edition, Directory of Social Change, 2000, London.

34 Karen Lowry Miller, 'The Teflon Shield', *Newsweek*, 12th March 2001, p36.

35 Mark Blaug, *Economic Theories, True or False? Essays in the History and Methodology of Economics*, Edward Elgar, Aldershot, 1990.

36 Tim Hames, 'Professional classes turn leftwards', *The Times*, 2nd March 2001, p24.

37 David Brooks, *Bobos in Paradise: The New Upper Class and How They Got There*, Simon & Schuster, New York, 2000.

38 David F. Murphy & David Mathew, *Nike & Global Labour Practices*, New Academy of Business, Bristol, January 2001, www.new-academy.ac.uk

39 Klein, op cit, 2000 p.361.

40 Idem.

41 Mark Blaug, *Economic Theory in Retrospect (Fifth Edition)*, Cambridge University Press, Cambridge, 1996, p262.

42 Naomi Klein, 'Between McWorld and Jihad', *The Guardian*, 27th October 2001, Guardian Weekend, p32.

43 For random examples see *Socialist Worker*, no 1737, 3rd March 2001 and *Workers Power*, issue 252, March 2001.

44 London Greenpeace (a), 'Who are London Greenpeace', published on *McSpotlight* web site.

45 For an account of the case see John Vidal, *McLibel: Burger Culture on Trial*, Macmillan, London, 1997; or David Hooper, *Reputations Under*

Fire, Warner Books (Little, Brown & Company), London, 2001.

46 London Greenpeace (a), op cit.

47 Idem.

48 Vidal, op cit, p337.

49 London Greenpeace (a), op cit.

50 Hooper, op cit, p160.

51 Vidal, op cit, p17.

52 See The Body Shop website, *www.thebodyshop.co.uk*, *www.bodyshop.com*

53 London Greenpeace (b), 'What's wrong with The Body Shop - a criticism of "green" consumerism.', published on *McSpotlight* website.

54 London Greenpeace (a), op cit.

55 Ian Hill & Shane Duffield, *Share Ownership - A Report on Ownership of Shares as at 31 December 2000*, Office for National Statistics, HMSO, London, 2001, p7.

56 Ibid, p9.

57 Idem.

58 Ibid, p8.

59 'Individual shareholders in the UK', Press Office, 15th April 2002, Proshare, *www.proshare.org*

60 Chris Ayres, 'Farewell to the American dream for life savings', *The Times*, 6th December 2001, p28.

61 David Rowan, 'Chumbawamba's tune turns the table on US car giant', *The Observer*, 27th January 2002, p11.

62 Ruckus Society website, *www.ruckus.org*

63 Alexander Cockburn & Jeffrey St. Clair, *5 Days That Shook the World - Seattle and Beyond*, Verso, London, 2000, p59.

64 Ruckus Society website, op cit.

65 Idem.

66 Turner Foundation website, 1999 grants, www.turnerfoundation.org

67 Julia Finch, 'Body Shop gains a new head - Roddicks step down as US team strives to make store chain desirable again', *The Guardian*, 13th February 2002.

68 Ruckus Society, ibid.

69 The Body Shop website, Body Shop Foundation, www.bodyshop.com

70 Anita Roddick, *Take It Personally - How Globalization Affects You and How To Fight Back*, Thorsons, An imprint of HarperCollins, London, 2001, p275.

71 Idem, p2.

72 Anita Roddick, *Business as Unusual - The Triumph of Anita Roddick*, Thorsons, An Imprint of HarperCollins, London, 2000.

73 UK May Day Monopoly Game Guide to Anti-Capitalist Actions on Tuesday 1st May 2001, *Global Action against Capitalism*, 2001.

74   Website of Patagonia, *www.patagonia.com*
75   Grace Bradberry, 'Classes in chaos', *The Times*, 25th July 2000, Times 2 pp3-4.
76   Website of Ben and Jerry, *www.benjerry.com*
77   Idem.
78   James Harding, 'Unilever funds anti-capitalists: Groups gain millions from Ben & Jerry takeover', *Financial Times*, 16th October 2001.
79   Idem.
80   www.benjerry.com, ibid.
81   Niall FitzGerald, 'Globalisation crucial to creation of just world', *The Times*, 12th November 2001, p23.
82   James Harding, ibid.
83   Website of Institute for Social Ecology, *www.social-ecology.org*
84   See Murray Bookchin's publication *Left Green Perspectives*, www.leftgreen.org
85   See Adbusters website, www.adbusters.org
86   Idem.
87   Kalle Lasn, Culture Jam - *How to Reverse America's Suicidal Consumer Binge - And Why We Must*, Quill, an imprint of HarperCollins, New York, 2000.
88   Publications and Media section of the Foundation for Deep Ecology website, www.deepecology.com
89   Doug Tompkins, *Remarks to the 2001 Land Trust Alliance Rally*, 2nd October 2001, www.lta.org
90   Jonathan Franklin & John Vidal, 'Baron Lands', *The Guardian*, Guardian Society, 23rd January 2002, pp8-9.
91   Naomi Klein, 'Hug Your Customer', *The Guardian*, 31st May 2001, p23.
92   Cockburn & St. Clair, ibid, pp58-59.
93   James Harding, 'Counter-Capitalism: Feeding the hands that bite', *www.ft.com*, 15th October 2001.
94   David Aaronovitch, 'Harry Potter and the Menace of Global Capitalism, *The Independent*, 28th September 2000.
95   George Monbiot, 'Business of Betrayal', *The Guardian*, 15th January 2002, p15.
96   Idem.
97   John Bray, 'Web Wars - NGOs, companies, and governments in an Internet-connected world', in Jem Bendell (ed.), *Terms for Endearment, Business, NGOs and Sustainable Development*, Greenleaf, Sheffield, 2000, pp56-60.
98   See the Burma Project website of the Soros Foundation, www.soros.org
99   See Burma Campaign UK website, www.burmacampaign.org.uk; 'Barbed-wire bra protest over Burma investment', *BBC News online*, 10th December 2001, www.news.bbc.co.uk

100 John Bray, op cit, p59.

101 Michael Griffin, *Reaping the Whirlwind - The Taliban Movement in Afghanistan*, Pluto Press, 2001, p181-182.

102 Ahmed Rashid, *Taliban - Islam, Oil and the New Great Game in Central Asia*, I B Tauris & Co, London, 2000, pp159-180.

103 Saeed Shah & Paul Waugh, 'Balfour Beatty pulls out of Turkish dam project', *The Independent*, 14th November 2001, p11; Roland Gribben, 'Balfour quits controversial Ilisu dam', *Daily Telegraph*, 14th November 2001, p35.

104 Mark Thomas, 'The proposed Ilisu dam is dead! We've Won!', *New Statesman*, 19th November 2001, p23.

105 'Swiss Bank quits Turkish dam project', *BBC News online*, 27th February 2002, www.news.bbc.co.uk

106 For an account of Greenpeace International's campaign against Shell see Mark Neal & Christie Davies, *The Corporation under Siege - Exposing the Devices used by Activists and Regulators in the Non-Risk Society*, Social Affairs Unit, London, 1998, pp22-25.

107 See Stop Esso Campaign web site, www.stopesso.com

108 Polly Toynbee, 'A Tiger out of your tank', *The Guardian*, 30th November 2001, p21.

109 Greenpeace International website, 'Greenpeace welcomes new policy commitment from IKEA', 24th November 1999, and other press releases on Greenpeace International website, www.greenpeace.org

110 George Monbiot and Jonathan Porritt, 'Does working with business compromise the environmentalists? A debate,' *The Ecologist*, September 2000, pp20-23.

111 Des Wilson, 'This juvenile posturing is for punks', *The Guardian*, 16th January 2002, p18.

112 Ibid, p23.

113 See PETA website, 'Annual Review 2000', www.peta-online.org

114 Andrew Clark, 'M&S bans Indian leather goods', *The Guardian*, 22nd June 2001, p23.

115 See PETA website, 'PETA to Coca-Cola: Dump Cruel, Racist Drink', www.peta-online.org

116 Paul Brown, 'Airlines refuse to carry Norway's whale exports', *The Guardian*, 10th June 2001.

117 Paul Kelso and Steven Morris, 'Haphazard army with the scent of victory', *The Guardian*, 18th January 2001, p5.

118 Jill Treanor, Steven Morris, and Andrew Clark, 'Huntingdon Life: facing collapse in 36 hours', *The Guardian*, 18th January 2001, p4.

119 Julia Finch, 'Drug firms threaten bank boycotts', *The Guardian*, 2nd May 2001.

120 Jill Treanor, 'Huntingdon backer denies it was forced to sell stake', *The Guardian*, 10th January 2002.

121   Polly Toynbee, 'Running scared - Huntingdon Life Sciences has been abandoned by cowards who fear an animal rights terror campaign', The Guardian, 17th January 2001.

122   Jeffrey M. Berry, The New Liberalism - The Rising Power of Citizen Groups, Brookings Institution, p131.

123   Ibid, p132.

124   Noreena Hertz, op. cit., 2001, p213.

125   Louise Jury, 'Benetton to apologise to US families over Death Row campaign.' The Independent, 19th June 2001, p5.

126   'What do you mean, chicken supreme?', The Economist, 13th January 2001, p34.

127   Klein, op cit, 2000, p422.

128   See Reebok website, Human Rights section, www.reebok.com

129   Mark Honigsbaum, 'GM martyr ignites global protest', The Guardian, 12th September 1999.

130   Klein, op cit, 2000, p188.

131   See websites for the FairTrade Foundation, Forest Stewardship Council, and Soil Association. www.fairtrade.org.uk; www.fscoax.org; www.soilassociation.org

132   Rowan Pelling, 'Good Vibrations', The Guardian, 21st November 2000.

133   Peter Lilley, Common Sense on Cannabis: The Conservative Case for Reform, Social Market Foundation, London, 2001.

134   Economist survey 'Legalise Drugs', The Economist, 26th June 2001.

135   Nick Paton Walsh and Gaby Hinsliff, 'Drug laws revolution set for UK', The Guardian, 16th February 2002.

136   Decca Aitkenhead, The Promised Land - Travels in search of the perfect E, Fourth Estate, London, 2002, pp20-21.

137   Thorsten Veblen, The Theory of the Leisure Class, first published 1899, Dover Publications, London, 1994.

138   Douglas Johnson, 'Pierre Bourdieu - Obituary', The Guardian, 28th January 2002, p18.

139   Pierre Bourdieu, Distinction - A Social Critique of the Judgement of Taste, Routledge, Kegan & Paul, London, 1986.

140   Eric Schlosser, Fast Food Nation - What The All-American Meal is Doing to the World, Allen Lane The Penguin Press, London, 2001, pp 13-28.

141   Ibid, p23.

142   Roddick, 2000, op cit, p37.

143   Lauren Mills, 'Credibility Gap', Sunday Telegraph, 18th November 2001.

144   The Economist, 8th September 2001, op cit, p27.

145   James Rolph Edwards, 'The Myth of Corporate Power', Liberty, January 2001, pp41-42.

146   Sarah Anderson and John Cavanagh, Top 200: The Rise of Corporate

Global Power, Institute for Policy Studies, Washington DC, 2000.

147 'Fortune 2001 Global 500', *Fortune*, 30th July 2001.

148 Martin Wolf, 'Countries still rule the world', *Financial Times*, 6th February 2002.

149 See Campaign for Real Ale web site, *www.camra.org.uk*

150 Farmers' Market East web site, 'Where are farmers' markets?', www.farmersmarketeast.org.uk

151 Nina Planck, *'The Way We Were: How to restore the link between farmers and everyone else'*, www.lfm.org.uk

152 *Human Development Report 2001 - Making New Technologies Work For Human Development*, Oxford University Press, New York, 2001.

153 Ibid, p9.

154 Ibid, p10, p22.

155 Ibid, p16.

156 *Globalization, Growth and Poverty: Building An Inclusive World Economy*, World Bank & Oxford University Press, New York, 2002.

157 David Dollar, *Globalization, Inequality and Poverty Since 1980*, World Bank Web site, November 2001. This is a research report commissioned for Globalization, Growth and Poverty, 2002.

158 Idem.

159 *Globalization, Growth & Poverty*, 2002.

160 Dollar, 2001.

161 Idem.

162 Edward M. Graham, *Fighting The Wrong Enemy - Anti-Global Activists and Multinational Enterprises*, Institute for International Economics, 2000, p93.

163 Ibid, p102.

164 Ibid, p101.

165 Charlotte Denny, 'Cheap labour, ruined lives', *The Guardian*, 16th February 2001.

166 Friedrich Engels, *The Condition of the Working Class in England*, First published 1845, Penguin Classics Edition, London, 1987, p51.

The Social Affairs Unit

'The Social Affairs Unit is famous for driving its coach and horses through the liberal consensus, scattering intellectual picket lines as it goes. It is equally famous for raising questions which strike most people most of the time as too dangerous or too difficult to think about.'

The Times

The Social Affairs Unit
Morley House
Regent Street
London W1B 3BB

www.socialaffairsunit.org.uk

SOME PUBLICATIONS FROM THE SOCIAL AFFAIRS UNIT

THE CORPORATION UNDER SIEGE
Exposing the devices used by activists and regulators in the non-risk society
Mark Neal & Christie Davies

WHAT HAS ETHICAL INVESTMENT TO DO WITH ETHICS?
Digby Anderson

CORPORATE IRRESPONSIBILITY
Is business appeasing anti-business activists?
Robert Halfon

NO MAN CAN SERVE TWO MASTERS
Shareholders versus stakeholders in the governance of companies
Joseph F Johnston

STAKEHOLDING
Betraying the corporation's objectives
Elaine Sternberg

GOOD COMPANIES DON'T HAVE MISSIONS
Digby Anderson

WHEN IS A CAT FAT?
A critical look at executive remuneration
Elaine Sternberg

THE MANY WAYS OF GOVERNANCE
Perspectives on the control of the firm
Martin Ricketts

AN AMERICAN LESSON FOR EUROPEAN COMPANY DIRECTORS
The emerging consensus in corporate governance
Joseph F Johnston

THE DICTIONARY OF DANGEROUS WORDS
compiled by Digby Anderson
"This book will shortly replace a university education.
And its cheaper" John Cleese

LOSING FRIENDS
Digby Anderson
"A Tour De Force" *National Review*

**FAKING IT: THE SENTIMENTALISATION OF MODERN
SOCIETY**
edited by Digby Anderson & Peter Mullen
"The more people who read this book the better"
Chris Woodhead in Sunday Telegraph

**GENTILITY RECALLED:
"MERE" MANNERS AND THE MAKING OF SOCIAL
ORDER**
edited by Digby Anderson
"I wanted to know why the world had changed so much and
I got the answer from Gentility Recalled"
Bernard Levin in *The Times*

ANOTHER COUNTRY
edited by Digby Anderson & Michael Mosbacher